Healing Our World

DAVID MORLEY

Fitzhenry & Whiteside

First published in paperback in 2008

Published in Canada by Fitzhenry & Whiteside, 195 Allstate Parkway, Markham, Ontario L3R 4T8

Published in the United States by Fitzhenry & Whiteside, 311 Washington Street, Brighton, Massachusetts 02135

www.fitzhenry.ca   godwit@fitzhenry.ca

10 9 8 7 6 5 4 3 2 1

Library and Archives Canada Cataloguing in Publication
Morley, David
    Healing our world : inside Doctors Without Borders / David Morley.
ISBN 978-1-55041-565-0 (bound) ISBN 978-1-55455-050-0 (pbk.)

    1. Doctors Without Borders (Association)—Juvenile literature.   2. Medical assistance—Juvenile literature.   3. War relief—-Juvenile literature.
4. Disaster relief—Juvenile literature.   I. Title.

RA390.A2M67 2006   j610.6'01   C2006-903251-3

U.S. Publisher Cataloging-in-Publication Data (Library of Congress Standards)
Morley, David.
    Healing our world : inside Doctors Without Borders / David Morley.
[112] p. : cm.

Summary: An inside look at a medical care agency.

ISBN-13: 978-1-55455-050-0 (pbk.)

1. Doctors Without Borders (Association). 2. Medical assistance. 3. Humanitarian assistance.
4. International relief. I. Title.

610.6/01 dc22   RA390.A2M675   2008

Fitzhenry & Whiteside acknowledges with thanks the Canada Council for the Arts, and the Ontario Arts Council for their support of our publishing program. We acknowledge the financial support of the Government of Canada through the Book Publishing Industry Development Program (BPIDP) for our publishing activities.

Design by Fortunato Design Inc.
Cover images courtesy of Steve Harris
Printed in Canada

Contents

INTRODUCTION

I WAS FINISHING UNIVERSITY and not sure what to do next when I heard that a family friend, who was a well-known advocate for human rights, was coming to town. His day would be filled with meetings, he told me, but he had time for a quick breakfast. So I flung on my jacket and my only tie and went to meet him at his hotel.

He worked for the Ontario Human Rights Commission, and perhaps, I thought, he could help me get a job there. He listened to me kindly as I shared my ideas about what was wrong with the world, and then he said, "You'll have lots of time to work in an office in the future, David." He reached into his pocket, pulled out a piece of paper, and wrote down a name and address. "First, you should volunteer overseas," he advised. He handed me the paper. "Here's a good place to apply. Contact Elizabeth at Pueblito."

So I took his advice, and nothing has been the same since. Pueblito accepted me to volunteer with street children in Central America. From there, I lived and worked with children in other parts of Latin America, raised money in Canada for international causes, became involved in international coalitions for children's rights, and for seven years, was lucky enough to serve as the executive director of the Canadian section of Médecins Sans Frontières, also known as Doctors Without Borders.

This book shares some experiences from my time with MSF—the work we do, what it's like to be on mission, and how, although we leave our homes with the idea of helping others, it seems we always return home enriched and awed by the kindness, determination, and strength of some of the poorest people in the world.

This collection of memories, reflections, and facts owes a great deal to many people, but I can name only a few of them here. My thanks go to Dr. Michael Schull, for his confidence and leadership;

v

Dr. Leslie Shanks, for her unwavering commitment to the ideals of MSF; Annik Chalifour, Tommi Laulajainen, Michèle Joanisse, and the outstanding staff of MSF Canada; Dr. Ocean, Mireille, Jean-Parfait, Luc, Branca, and other remarkable MSF national staff members I have worked with around the world; the two Lindas–Linda Biesenthal, for editing and shaping my ideas into a coherent form, and Linda Nagy, who supported this book from the beginning; Clea Kahn, Joe Belliveau, Eva Lam, Dr. Saleem Kassam, Ralph Heeschen, Dr. Esther Mtumbuka, Riekje Elema, Dr. Simon Collins, Lilliane Archambault-Cyr, Joost Van Montfort, Dr. James Orbinski, Steve Cornish, and the hundreds of volunteers who have put their ideals and beliefs on the line by serving in every corner of the globe; my sons, Nicholas and Alexander, whose questions about the wider world and interest in the lives of people far beyond our borders helped inspire this book, and, of course, Bruce McLeod, for that eventful breakfast.

And as for Elizabeth, the woman I applied to for my first overseas volunteer position? Two years after we met we were married, and it is to her, for her patience and support through all my traveling, for her intelligence, insights, understanding, and love, that I dedicate this book.

PART 1

About Doctors Without Borders

DURING MY SEVEN YEARS as executive director of the Canadian section of Médecins Sans Frontières (MSF)—also known as Doctors Without Borders—I talked with many students who wanted to know how our organization worked, where we went on our missions, what we did when we got there, and about the lives of the people we were there to help.

The genuine and compassionate curiosity of these students inspired the first part of this book. Here I've tried to answer their questions in more detail and to give a more complete picture of the way MSF works.

Humanitarian action is more than simple generosity, simple charity … We aim to enable individuals to regain their rights and dignity as human beings. As an independent volunteer association, we are committed to bringing direct medical aid to people in need. But we act not in a vacuum, and we speak not into the wind, but with a clear intent to assist, to provoke change, or to reveal injustice …

Our volunteers and staff live and work among people whose dignity is violated every day. These volunteers choose freely to use their liberty to make the world a more bearable place. Despite grand debates on world order, the act of humanitarianism comes down to one thing: individual human beings reaching out to others who find themselves in the most difficult circumstances. One bandage at a time, one suture at a time, one vaccination at a time.

—JAMES ORBINSKI, *International president of Médecins Sans Frontières/Doctors Without Borders, accepting the Nobel Peace Prize, December 1999*

CHAPTER 1

The World Is Our Emergency Room

9T IS EASY to feel hopeless when images of human tragedy fill the TV screen. Natural disasters, civil wars, starving children—they seem to roll on without stopping.

But when you look closer, the picture changes. You see people caring for each other, not just killing each other. You see people helping, not just destroying. That's what humanitarianism is all about—people caring for people who are suffering, people working together to build a better world for everyone.

Many people and many organizations are trying to make the world a better place. One of those organizations is Médecins Sans Frontières, known in English as Doctors Without Borders, and known to its volunteers by the letters of its French name—MSF. MSF is the world's largest independent medical-humanitarian organization.

Every year, MSF brings medical care to people in more than 70 countries. We go where the need for medical care is greatest, setting up emergency rooms in tents, running mobile clinics to treat people injured in earthquakes and attacked in civil wars, helping victims of AIDS and other diseases, and feeding malnourished children in refugee camps in forgotten corners of the world.

A HUMANITARIAN WORLD

Humanitarians believe in a world where everyone in the human family shares the same rights. That includes the right to live with dignity, the right to receive medical assistance, and the right to all of life's necessities—food and clean water, shelter and security, medical care and education. Humanitarians also believe they have a responsibility to care for people who are struggling to survive. That means taking action—reaching out a helping hand to victims of disease, disaster, poverty, and war.

In Our World ...

- 1 billion people live without clean drinking water.
- 2 billion people live without safe sanitation facilities.
- 1.8 million children die each year from diseases caused by dirty water and poor sanitation.
- 40.3 million people are infected with HIV, including 2 million young people aged 15–24.
- 14 million children have lost at least one parent to AIDS.
- 90 percent of HIV-positive people in poor countries have no access to the antiretroviral medicines that are used to treat the disease in rich countries.
- 500,000 children die of measles each year, most in developing countries where they have no access to effective vaccines.
- more than 1 million people die from malaria each year because they have no access to treatment.
- 25 million people were displaced in their own countries because of war or human rights violations in 2004.
- 25 million people were victims of natural disasters in 2004.
- 1 billion people do not have enough food to survive.
- more than 8 million people die each year because of poverty.

Source: United Nations

Mexico

Cuba   Haiti

Guatemala   Honduras
El Salvador   Nicaragua
Costa Rica   Venezuela

Colombia

Ecuador

Peru   B r a z i l

Bolivia

Médecins Sans Frontières:

Missions Around the World

Born in Biafra

The idea for Médecins Sans Frontières was born in Biafra. In 1967 Colonel Ojukwu, leader of the Ibo people in the eastern region of Nigeria, declared independence and called the new state Biafra. A brutal civil war began. In an all-out effort to win the war, the Nigerian army attacked farms and cut off food supplies to Biafrans.

In 1968 a group of French doctors volunteered with the Red Cross to help the victims of the war in Biafra. The doctors were horrified by the atrocities they witnessed—food kept away from starving children, civilians killed mercilessly, medical centers deliberately attacked.

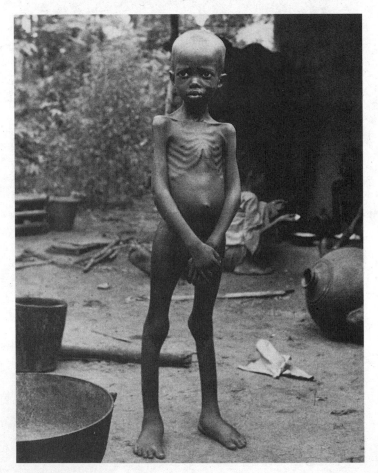

In North America and Europe, TV screens were filled with pictures of starving Biafran children, and people began raising money to send food and medicine. Despite this help, more than a million people died, mostly from diseases related to malnutrition.

As they treated the victims of the war, the French doctors became angry and frustrated. They had signed an agreement with the Red Cross promising to stay neutral and not take sides in the civil war. It was only under this condition of neutrality that the government of Nigeria would let the Red Cross doctors into the country.

But one of the French doctors, Bernard Kouchner, could not accept neutrality at all costs. "By keeping silent," he said later, "we doctors were accomplices in the systematic massacre of a population." Kouchner did not want to be part of a replay of the Holocaust. During the Second World War, when Red Cross doctors learned about the gas chambers in Auschwitz, they did not speak out, fearing that if they did the German authorities would not let them help the prisoners of war.

When Dr. Kouchner returned to France, he broke his oath of silence with the Red Cross and openly condemned the brutality of the Nigerian government. He organized public protests in Paris, trying to make the world pay attention to the plight of the Biafran people.

By 1970 the Biafran war was over, but Kouchner and his friends were just beginning. They started making plans for a new humanitarian group of medical volunteers. Their volunteers would provide emergency medical care to people in danger around the world, but they would also go one step further. They would put their patients ahead of politics. They would insist on the right of victims to receive medical aid and their own right to provide medical care for people caught in the middle of a conflict—no matter what political authorities might say. And they would also insist on speaking out when they witnessed human rights violations.

The decision to speak out broke an important rule of humanitarian aid. Staying neutral in a conflict—which means saying nothing against governments and military forces—was one of the fundamental principles of the Red Cross. The Red Cross argued that humanitarian workers had to stay neutral in order to negotiate their way into war zones and treat civilians caught in conflicts.

Sans Frontières/Without Borders

In 1971 the doctors who had worked in Biafra joined another fledgling humanitarian organization, Secours Médical Français (French Medical Relief). It had been started the year before by Raymond Borel and his colleagues at a French medical journal. Borel had recruited volunteer doctors and sent them to treat the survivors of the Bhola Cyclone, which had killed 500,000 people in Bangladesh. The experience of these volunteer doctors highlighted the need for a humanitarian group that could act independently and avoid the red tape that slowed down large organizations.

Both Kouchner and Borel wanted an organization that would respond quickly to medical crises around the world and that would put patients ahead of politics. So, on December 20, 1971, Médecins Sans Frontières was born in Paris. *Sans Frontières* in the new organization's name was significant. It reflected MSF's commitment to ignore national borders and bring emergency medical help to people who needed it, no matter where they lived.

The issue of neutrality, however, was a source of disagreement. Kouchner advocated speaking out when volunteers witnessed human rights violations. The experience of Borel's volunteers told them that silence was a price worth paying in order to get medical care to victims of war. When the two groups decided to join forces, Dr. Kouchner's volunteers from Biafra reluctantly agreed that neutrality and staying silent would be the rule of Médecins Sans Frontières.

Bernard Kouchner carries a Vietnamese refugee to safety, 1979.

MSF Charter

Médecins Sans Frontières offers assistance to populations in distress, to victims of natural or man-made disasters and to victims of armed conflict, without discrimination and irrespective of race, religion, creed, or political affiliation.

Médecins Sans Frontières observes neutrality and impartiality in the name of universal medical ethics and the right to humanitarian assistance and demands full and unhindered freedom in the exercise of its functions.

Médecins Sans Frontières' volunteers promise to honor their professional code of ethics and to maintain complete independence from all political, economic, and religious powers.

As volunteers, members are aware of the risks and dangers of the missions they undertake and have no right to compensation for themselves or their beneficiaries other than that which Médecins Sans Frontières is able to afford them.

The Early Years

French doctors quickly signed up as volunteers for the new organization. They provided emergency medical care when the city of Managua, Nicaragua, was destroyed by an earthquake in 1972, and when Hurricane Fifi destroyed villages and killed 8,000 people in Honduras in 1974. These first volunteers hitched rides on relief flights and opened clinics in tents. But their help was limited. Many established humanitarian aid agencies called MSF's volunteers "medical hippies."

Things started to change in 1976. Civil war was destroying the beautiful city of Beirut in Lebanon, and MSF sent 56 volunteers to serve in a beleaguered hospital in one of the city's war-torn neighborhoods. This work earned the praise of *Time* magazine, which called MSF "an extraordinary organization." For the first time, MSF ran a serious fund-raising campaign in France, with the slogan: "We have 2 billion people in our waiting room." MSF was growing up.

The need for MSF was growing, too. Conflicts were erupting in Angola and Mozambique in southern Africa, in Ethiopia and Somalia, in Cambodia in southeast Asia, in Nicaragua and El Salvador in Central America. These wars forced hundreds of thousands of people to flee from their homes. In 1979, the number of refugees in the world stood at 5.7 million, and by 1985 that number had doubled.

Refugee camps started to spring up all over the world. And with the increasing financial independence that had come from its fund-raising campaigns, MSF was able to respond. Soon small MSF clinics in tents could be found in refugee camps from Honduras to Thailand.

In 1979 the Soviet Union invaded Afghanistan. MSF knew that the Soviets would never allow outsiders into the country, so the volunteers rode donkeys up over secret mountain passes to bring medical care to Afghans. Five years later, in Ethiopia, the issue of neutrality and speaking out was once again on MSF's agenda.

Guiding Principles of MSF

Independence

MSF is independent of outside influences. Unlike any other international aid agency, MSF sets a limit on the amount of government funding it will accept—because all too often government money comes with strings attached. About 75 percent of MSF's funds for

its missions comes from individual donors. That means MSF has the independence it needs to be able to respond quickly and where it feels the need is greatest.

Impartiality

MSF provides medical care based on the need of the people who are suffering, regardless of race, religion, or political borders.

Neutrality

MSF never take sides with military forces or rebels. But when its volunteers witness serious abuses of fundamental human rights, MSF speaks out.

Proximity

MSF works closely with patients. Volunteers on mission serve people directly, and that means providing front-line, hands-on medical care to the people who need it.

Voluntarism

MSF is a movement of volunteers. Their only motivation is to help people who are suffering.

Speaking Out

In 1984 a drought followed by famine struck Ethiopia, and the world rallied to help. Live Aid, the first globally televised rock benefit concert, raised money and awareness, and the songs "Tears Are Not Enough," "We Are the World," and "Do They Know It's Christmas?" raised millions of dollars in famine relief. Western governments joined in, and soon more aid dollars were heading to Ethiopia.

Using the foreign aid dollars it was receiving from around the world, the government of Ethiopia began to move people away from the drought-stricken region. The government claimed it was just moving people to a more fertile part of the country, but villagers were forced to leave their homes against their will, families were separated, and often the places they were sent to were no better than the places they had left behind.

MSF was in Ethiopia setting up feeding centers and providing medical assistance for people suffering from malnutrition. It seemed clear to MSF's team that the Ethiopian government was using the famine as a cover. It was moving people away from the north of the country, where the provinces of Eritrea and Tigray were fighting a war of independence, and into the south. It amounted to an ethnic reshuffling. According to some MSF reports, these forced transfers were killing more people than the famine, but foreign governments and other agencies said nothing.

Finally, in December 1985, MSF publicly denounced the Ethiopian government, and the MSF volunteers spoke out against the treatment of the villagers from the north who had been forced to move. As expected, the government of Ethiopia expelled MFS's volunteers. But neither their work nor their speaking out had been in vain. Within a few months, the United States, Great Britain, and other countries that had been sending large amounts of aid money told the Ethiopian government that the forced movement of the villagers in the north had to stop if aid money was to continue, and the Ethiopian government complied.

A Good Idea Grows

In the early 1980s, the MSF idea was growing more popular, and the organization expanded. New branches opened up, first in Switzerland and Belgium, and then in Holland and Spain. By the early 1990s, MSF had offices in 19 countries on three continents.

More offices brought more resources, and MSF was able to invest in improving itself. In order to get medical supplies to its missions as quickly as possible, MSF started producing pre-packaged emergency kits that were ready to go at a moment's notice. Money was spent on research to improve MSF's medical treatments in the field. MSF also invested in fund-raising, and focused on donations from individual donors. That meant that, unlike most humanitarian aid agencies, MSF would not be dependent on the political whims of governments and their foreign aid budgets.

MSF volunteers unloading emergency kits after the tsunami hit southeast Asia in 2004. MSF came up with the idea of assembling and storing kits filled with emergency supplies that are ready for immediate transport to missions anywhere in the world.

With these improvements, MSF volunteers were able to help victims in some of the most desperate and dangerous places in the world—in Kurdistan after the first war in Iraq in 1991; in the Balkans during the war that broke up Yugoslavia; and in Rwanda during the genocide in 1994. The horrors of Rwanda—when 800,000 people were killed in 100 days of ethnic violence—was a stark reminder of the limits of humanitarian work. "You can't stop a genocide with doctors"—this was the cry of MSF as it called for military intervention to stop the slaughter.

How MSF Is Organized

MSF has national offices, called sections, in 19 countries. Many people think one strong, global office would make it easier to co-ordinate our activities, but we do not. We think that an organization that is too centralized leads to too many rules and too much bureaucracy, which can stifle an individual's ability to react when faced with a crisis in the field.

MSF's sections are organized into five sub-groups, called operational portfolios:

- Operational Center Brussels includes Belgium, Denmark, Hong Kong, Italy, Norway, and Sweden.
- Operational Center Amsterdam includes Holland, Germany, Canada, and the United Kingdom.
- Operational Center Paris includes Australia, France, Japan, and the United States.
- Operational Center Geneva includes Austria and Switzerland.
- Operational Center Barcelona includes Spain and Greece.

Within each of the national sections, there are people who carry out the important jobs of fund-raising, finding good volunteers, raising awareness about humanitarian crises, and managing our medical projects.

Into the New Century

In the dying days of 1999, the world was delighted to learn that MSF had been awarded the Nobel Peace Prize. It was a popular choice, even though MSF volunteers didn't consider themselves to be members of a peace organization.

> *"The peace Alfred Nobel was thinking of when he established the prize was a peace that is rooted in people's hearts and minds. By showing each victim a human face, by showing respect for his or her human dignity, the fearless and selfless aid worker creates hope for peace ..."*
>
> **—Nobel Peace Prize Committee**

On December 10, 1999, James Orbinski, the Canadian doctor who was serving as MSF's international president, accepted the Nobel Peace Prize in Oslo, Norway: "As we accept this extraordinary honor, we want to thank the Nobel Committee for its affirmation of the right to humanitarian assistance around the globe. For its affirmation of the road MSF has chosen to take: to remain outspoken, passionate and deeply committed to its core principles of volunteerism, impartiality, and its belief that every person deserves both medical assistance and the recognition of his or her humanity."

Dr. Orbinski also laid out the next challenge facing MSF. "More than 90 percent of all death and suffering from infectious diseases occurs in the developing world. Some of the reasons that people die from diseases like AIDS, TB, sleeping sickness, and other tropical diseases is that life-saving essential medicines are too expensive, are not available because they are not seen as financially viable, or because there is virtually no new research and development for priority tropical diseases. This market failure is our next challenge."

In the first years of the twenty-first century, MSF has continued along the path proposed by Dr. Orbinski. The organization has focused on people victimized by wars and people victimized by infectious diseases that they are too poor to prevent.

Dr. James Orbinski accepting the Nobel Peace Prize in 1999

THE NOBEL PEACE PRIZE

Early morning phone calls usually bring bad news, so I expected the worst when the phone rang to wake me up in my Toronto home at 5:30 that dark morning in October 1999. But I was wrong.

The voice came down the line. "MSF has just won the Nobel Peace Prize. CTV will have a car at your house in 20 minutes so you can talk about it on national television." Now that woke me up.

That day and the ones that followed were a blur of excitement as MSF volunteers became, for a moment, the toast of the world.

But as the time went on, and much to my surprise, winning the Nobel Peace Prize became a bittersweet experience. Here is something I wrote in the days right after the announcement when I was serving as executive director of MSF Canada.

David Morley in Zambia

This has been a wonderfully exhilarating affirmation of our work. It is a recognition that ordinary people willing to go to the sad, desolate, and forgotten places in the world play a vital role in building world peace. It is recognition that peace needs more than the politicians to broker the deals—it needs countless individuals to carry out acts of kindness and help rebuild peace when there has been injustice and war. The Nobel Prize recognizes the importance of humanitarian ideals and the dignity of the victims who suffer needlessly because of war. It celebrates our independence from civil and military authorities. To have all of these beliefs and actions affirmed is heady stuff indeed.

On the other hand, children in Angola are still threatened by measles and we can't get the vaccines there in time to save them all. In Sierra Leone, we provided help to the innocent victims of the war whose hands and feet had been brutally chopped off, but we couldn't give them back their limbs. Women in Congo-Brazzaville are still being violated in horrific numbers and we haven't been able to stop it. And every morning, in refugee camps around the world, our field volunteers wake up to the same sights and sounds they saw when they fell asleep exhausted from a hard day's work.

Nevertheless, we should celebrate. I remember the words of a man in a refugee camp in Central America as he talked about international relief workers. "You come here to help, but if you don't celebrate our small triumphs, if you don't see the lives we have saved as well as the lives we have yet to save, then you won't last. If you want to be with us for the long haul, then celebrate with us, too."

This is a chance to celebrate the human spirit. To celebrate the resilience of children and mothers in a Mozambique refugee camp who can sing and play despite their atrocious wounds. To celebrate the commitment of humanitarian workers from around the world who make a difference every day. To celebrate the financial donations made by people who cannot be on the front lines, but who want to participate in some way.

So I think about it again. The Nobel Peace Prize is worth celebrating. It is a great honor for all the people committed to humanitarian relief. The Peace Prize Committee says MSF won because of its fundamental principle that "all disaster victims, whether the disaster is natural or human in origin, have a right to professional assistance, given as quickly and efficiently as possible. National boundaries and political circumstances or sympathies must have no influence on who is to receive humanitarian help. By maintaining a high degree of independence, the organization has succeeded in living up to these ideals."

Since this is why we received this honor, we must not let ourselves be lulled into silence. The killing fields and refugee camps seem the same today as they did before October 15, 1999, but perhaps in 10 years we will see this as a pivotal moment in recognizing the global importance of humanitarian ideals, humanitarian action, and humanitarian law.

There is a primary school in Toronto where the children have been particularly active fund-raisers for MSF. When they heard about the Nobel Peace Prize, they ran around the school calling out "We won! We won!" Maybe that's the point of this year's Nobel Peace Prize—we all win when humanitarian principles are celebrated and honored.

When I tell friends at home in Canada about my missions with MSF, they often say to me, "It must be so depressing." But it doesn't feel depressing.

Yes, there are many terrible things happening in the world—natural disasters, civil wars, the horrors of AIDS, refugee camps filled with hungry children. But at least with MSF, I get a chance to do something. I am with an organization built to act, to try to make things better for people who are suffering and need medical care.

Volunteers with MSF don't have to sit by helplessly, wondering what on earth we can do. In the face of disaster, we can respond. The gift of action is ours.

—DAVID MORLEY

CHAPTER 2

Volunteers in the Field

 VERY YEAR MSF sends about 3,000 volunteers on emergency medical missions around the world. We call these volunteers "ex-pats" (short for ex-patriates), because they leave behind their countries, their families, and their regular jobs to take on the hard work of caring for people suffering from hunger, violence, and disease.

Ex-pats travel to remote villages in Africa to bring health care to people who have none and new medicines to people who have AIDS, malaria, or TB. They set up feeding centers in refugee camps to treat children who are sick and dying from malnutrition. They find ways of providing clean water and sanitation to victims of natural disasters. They pitch surgery tents in war zones to save civilians caught in crossfire or deliberately attacked.

On MSF missions, every ex-pat becomes part of an international team of volunteers who come from many different parts of the world, with many different skills. The one thing they all share is a passion to care for—and about—people who need humanitarian help.

Not Just Doctors

Many people think that only doctors work with MSF, but ex-pats come from all walks of life and bring an array of skills and talents to each mission. In their regular lives, they have planted trees, fixed motorcycles, worked in the Far North, at youth shelters in inner cities, in classrooms and emergency rooms. When MSF is setting up a refugee camp in a place without electricity, running a TB clinic in the middle of

Simon and Marissa going to work in Congo, 2004.

a shanty town, or crossing front lines to get medical care to people trapped by war, it needs a team that can do just about everything.

About a third of MSF's ex-pats are non-medical volunteers. They are the people who handle the logistics of a mission, which means organizing, maintaining, and moving people and supplies. They keep our land cruisers running, set up latrines, and make sure that a mission has the bandages, medicines, beds, and everything else it needs. People who are good with numbers handle the money that goes in and out of a mission. Engineers help build water and sanitation systems and design cholera centers. Missions set up in war zones have people who alert us when a platoon of soldiers is on its way or some new political situation threatens the security of our patients.

Another third of our ex-pats come from jobs in the health care professions. On some missions, mental health specialists form part of the MSF team to assist people shattered by disaster and war. Epidemiologists join missions in Africa to study the patterns of infectious diseases—like malaria, sleeping sickness, and measles—in order to help the MSF team better understand and combat outbreaks. Lab technicians study the results of blood work when the mission is screening for AIDS and infectious diseases. They may also train local health care workers, showing them how to read slides and set up their own labs. At the heart of MSF's missions are the hundreds of nurses who care for patients, monitor their progress, comfort their families, and teach their communities how to deal with public health issues.

Only a third of our ex-pat volunteers are doctors. They include general practitioners, surgeons, anesthetists, and specialists in tropical diseases and public health. The purpose of every MSF mission is to ensure that people who need medical care get to see a doctor, and for many of them, it is their first time.

The Head of Mission has overall responsibility for the projects in a country, and the other members of the Country Management Team have responsibility for the main areas of our work—medical, logistical, and financial. These are usually people who have had many years of experience working overseas. They supervise the international volunteers and national staff and make sure we get the medical and human resources to the right place at the right time—not always an easy task in places where there is no electricity to run hospitals, no banking system to get easy access to money, and often no functioning government. But that, of course, is part of the challenge.

First Missioners

About 1,000 of MSF's volunteers are new every year. We call them "first missioners." That means that one-third of our volunteers are having the most profound experience of their lives. They are seeing for the first time the ravages of war, lives devastated in earthquakes, the horrors of the AIDS pandemic.

First missioners provide MSF with new eyes and new commitment. They stop MSF from turning into just another international organization filled with people who have seen so many disasters that it becomes harder to respond with empathy and compassion.

First missioners can still be shocked at what they see at those moments when old-time MSFers will say, "You think this is bad. You should have seen it at my mission three years ago." The first missioners can be the conscience of MSF, reminding us all of how we felt when we were first on mission—how we were going to change the world.

MSF volunteers stop for breakfast on Highway 1 in Congo, 2004.

VOLUNTEERING WITH MSF

MSF needs volunteers who combine a passion for humanitarian work with the skills it takes to operate an emergency medical mission in the field. Volunteers come from all over the world, from many different backgrounds and work experiences. The youngest are in their twenties, the oldest in their seventies. Some people discover MSF halfway through their careers. Others know they want to work for MSF in high school and set their goals for humanitarian work.

While there are no absolute criteria that all volunteers must meet, these are some of the things that MSF looks for when recruiting new volunteers:

- at least two years of work experience in a medical field (doctors, nurses, midwives); or in a technical field (water and sanitation, mechanics, communication, construction); or as a manager, project co-ordinator, or administrator
- some experience living or working with different cultures
- ability to speak either French or English and another language
- flexibility to leave for a mission on short notice and serve for at least nine months
- good social and communication skills
- ability to work as part of an international team
- commitment, compassion, and courage

The first step in the recruitment process is an application, which can be found on MSF web sites. (In Canada, the web site is www.msf.ca; in the U.S., the web site is www.doctorswithout borders.org.) The applications are considered by human resources officers in MSF's national offices. Applicants who look promising go through a face-to-face interview, and if the fit of skills and passion seems right, they are sent on a training course. When their skills are needed on a mission, the volunteers go to the field as first missioners. MSF pays for travel and living expenses and provides volunteers with an allowance.

National Staff

As ex-pats working in the field, we know that the real heroes are the national staff, the people on the team who live in the country where MSF has set up its mission.

About 12,000 national staff work side by side with the 3,000 ex-pats sent on MSF missions each year. They include doctors, nurses, logisticians, warehouse keepers, carpenters, engineers, drivers, translators, guards, and cleaners. They know the country, traditions, and customs in a way we foreign ex-pats never will, and they know how to get things done.

In war zones, MSF tries to hire national staff from all sides of the conflict. This helps MSF retain its neutrality and shows that it is possible for people to work together rather than kill each other.

Medical staff in Congo, 2004

When I think of national staff members I have worked with, I think of Mireille, a nurse from the Republic of Congo who spent her vacation in our clinic looking after patients. There's Dorothy in Kalabo, a community health worker whose quiet efficiency kept our clinic running. There's Patrick in Sierra Leone, who survived the civil war—just barely—and worked with MSF to help build peace. There's Jean-Barnabé, the almost invisible but always resourceful driver who shepherds MSF first-timers through the chaos and rigmarole of Brazzaville airport.

And I think of the gentle voice of Dr. Ocean, a Congolese doctor I worked with in the Congo, where the civil war had robbed people of their homes, farms, schools, and hospitals. In charge of the national medical staff, Dr. Ocean is a compassionate man who cares deeply about the health and dignity of his patients. He is also a courageous man, who challenged his own government for using cheap, ineffective medicines to treat malaria and sleeping sickness.

"It is good to have you here with us," Dr. Ocean told me. "It shows that the outside world hasn't totally forgotten us. And if you come all the way here to help, then it gives us hope and more desire to help, too. And hope and desire are good things to have when you're stuck in a conflict like ours."

A vaccination team at work at an MSF clinic in Afghanistan

Voices of Volunteers

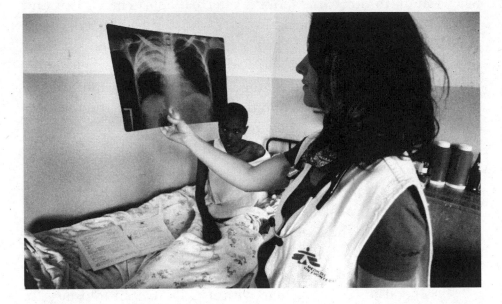

EVA LAM: Lab Technician

When Eva Lam was in high school in Toronto, she heard about MSF and knew that was what she wanted to do. But she liked research, too, and went on to become a research scientist. Her career took her to some of the biggest hospitals in Canada, but Eva never forgot her dream of volunteering in Africa.

Eva wasn't sure how someone with her skills as a researcher would fit in at MSF. But since she uses a microscope in her research, she became a laboratory technician for MSF and set up an important study on ACT (artemisinin-based combination therapy), a new medicine used to combat malaria.

Malaria is one of the biggest killers of children in the world—and the biggest health problem faced by MSF. The medicine used in most countries is out of date and no longer cures people, but ACT can cure a patient's malaria in three days and costs just 60 cents.

The World Health Organization and governments of both rich and poor countries were slow to accept that malaria could be beaten, so MSF decided to use research to show how it could be done. That's where Eva's skills came in. She went to Kailahun, a village in Sierra Leone, an African country torn apart by 10 years of civil war.

"I liked Kailahun. It was right in the middle of the bush, but the United Nations had peacekeepers there, and they had ice cream! I taught our national staff how to read the slides. And once you learn to read a slide in a microscope, it's like riding a bicycle—you never forget. The hardest part is taking the blood from the patient."

Coming home after her project in Sierra Leone was hard for Eva. "Friends at home think about which set of dishes to eat off for dinner, while my friends in Africa think about where or how they can get food for their family. People like us who have been volunteers have to let people in the rich countries know that there is so much more happening in the world than they see on TV."

So Eva has gone back to Africa, and will stay there for a while. "It's easy to find a job, but it's not easy to find a job that makes you happy. Africa draws me with an invisible force. Once you have been here, it's in your blood, whether you like it or not. And since MSF doesn't rely on government money, we can go where the need is greatest, not where a government tells us to go. That means I can make the most difference in people's lives."

CLEA KAHN: Logistician

Life with a comedy troupe. Life with MSF. That is how things have gone for Clea Kahn. Sometimes she can't tell the difference.

"Being a stage manager for *Just for Laughs* and being a logistician for MSF have a lot in common," she says. "You have to make sure that everything is where it's supposed to be when it's supposed to be there. The conditions are different, though."

In Sri Lanka, Clea organized things behind the scenes to make sure that medicines and hospital equipment could get across the front lines during the civil war. "In a war the fighters consider almost anything as a military supply, so they were even suspicious when we tried to get painkillers across the front lines, because they thought the other side would use them to help soldiers." Her experience in theater came in handy when she gave local health workers some drama training so they could put on plays to help the civilians caught in the war cope with the stress of an unbearable situation. "On one side, you had the government laying siege to a whole region, and on the other, you had rebels extorting money from the civilians they controlled."

From Sri Lanka, Clea went to Bangladesh, where MSF ran medical programs for refugees from Burma. The government and the United Nations wanted the refugees to return to Burma, but they were afraid to go back. So, as well as overseeing MSF's medical programs, Clea kept an eye on the authorities to make sure that the rights of the refugees were not ignored. And she learned that having outsiders watching a situation helped make it a little better. That was also what she found later when she was helping refugees from Darfur in Chad. "The Janjaweed militia would not attack when foreigners were present. Having outside eyes makes people safer."

For Clea, protection is the most important issue facing refugees. "All countries have signed agreements about what governments and militias are allowed to do. But what happens to the weakest people in situations when there is no law? You have to tell the people with guns that there is such a thing as International Humanitarian Law, that people have rights, that fighters can't just do whatever they want to do. Refugees need protection, and when we are there, delivering our medical services, our presence provides them with some of that."

RALPH HEESCHEN: Engineer

Ralph Heeschen was running a successful motorcycle dealership in Germany when his life changed. It was 1994. Shocked by the pictures he saw on TV from the genocide in Rwanda, he knew that he had to do something.

"I had been to Africa before. Right after university, I went to Somalia and I saw it all—the refugee camps, the suffering, and the gracious hospitality of the Africans. I knew I would have to go back." Ralph did go back, first to Rwanda, then to Burundi, Congo, and Sudan.

But what does a motorcycle dealer do for MSF? For someone with Ralph's mechanical skills, there's lots to do. Rigging up lighting for an operating theater in a shot-up hospital, making cars run when the right parts are hundreds of kilometers away, cobbling together water filters to make dirty water clean. "It becomes so natural to improvise because you don't have the right materials," Ralph says. "You can't sit still and wait, you have to go ahead and use your brain and experiment. And the local people have so much to teach. Just watch them repair a flat tire—they tear some rubber from a discarded tire and sew the patch on the wheel." It may be bumpy, but it works.

Driving in our land cruisers to make sure that electrical and water systems in the clinics are working often means going back and forth across military check-points, negotiating with men with guns who control a region. "I think we have the MSF shield," Ralph says. "The idealism, the fact we are just helping people, this gives me the assurance that we will be okay."

But often it is easier for the ex-pat volunteers than it is for the national staff. "Once, we were crossing the front lines with a truck and a land cruiser and everything around us went up in flames," Ralph recalls. "We volunteers were okay, but our national staff people were in danger if the soldiers saw them.

But we couldn't go back, so all the national staff got in the middle of the truck, and we foreigners sat closer to the windows so the soldiers could only see us and we made it through all right."

Ralph smiles. "Working and caring for people makes me happy. I can use my hands and my brain to improvise and build. You make friends, you give and take—when you give, you will be given to. I have learned so much from the Africans. I hope I have taught some things, too, but I know I have made good friends."

ESTHER MTUMBUKA: Doctor

"I loved math in high school, and I wanted to be an engineer. But in my last year I started to like biology, so that's when I decided to switch to medicine." It was not the usual route for a girl growing up in Tanzania in eastern Africa, and Esther was one of only seven women in her class.

After she became a doctor, Esther kept striving. "I could see that our underfunded medical system in Tanzania was not able to help enough people, and that in the Western world, public health had made the biggest difference in improving health. But we didn't have public health courses in Tanzania, so I went from embassy to embassy, trying to see if I could get a scholarship." Eventually Esther won a scholarship to Holland to study public health.

When she was in Europe, Esther heard about MSF and volunteered to become an HIV/AIDS doctor in Zambia. As an African woman, Esther has certain advantages. "I understand more about the culture, even though it is not exactly like mine. I can pick things up faster than most volunteers. But I don't think the patients accept me any differently than they do the other volunteers. What matters to them is how you approach them."

Esther was amazed at how much of a difference MSF can make in the lives of people in just a year. "Before, with no treatment possible, it was hard for anyone to admit they were HIV-positive. Now we have a group of people in the district who can talk in public about being HIV-positive, and they are talking to the District Health Center to make sure they get the drugs they need. Now other people are coming to us asking to be tested for HIV. People feel there is hope. If they are tested and they are HIV-positive, they know there is some hope.

"Now that we have the medicine to treat AIDS, I can think of AIDS in a calmer way. Back in Tanzania, when I told someone they were HIV-positive, it was a death sentence. Now they can have hope. When I put someone on antiretroviral medication to treat AIDS, within two or three weeks their face becomes radiant. This is the best reward."

RIEKJE ELEMA: Nurse

"I knew when I was a very young girl in Holland that I wanted to be a nurse," says Riekje Elema. "Why? I just liked looking after people."

After a holiday in Africa, Riekje knew she wanted to do her nursing overseas. She applied to MSF, was accepted as a volunteer, and waited to be sent on a mission. "I got a phone call on a Friday. 'Can you go to northern Uganda next week?'"

"When I got to Kampala, the capital of Uganda, I was told we were going to set up a program for 25,000 displaced people. There was lots of fighting between the army and rebels. When we reached the end of the paved highway, we stopped and put a big MSF flag on our land cruiser. 'Why are you doing that?' I asked. My head of mission replied, 'So the rebels know who we are.'"

Nobody else was on the road. Nobody walking. Nobody driving. My God, Riekje thought, where am I going? What is this place? But once they reached the town and started working, things felt better.

"We all learned quickly. We were running a surgical program and had seven small clinics. We would go to the clinics, set up a table, and there would be a line-up of 200 people—people who hadn't had health care in such a long time. People had lost their cattle because of the civil war, so many of the children were suffering from kwashiorkor, severe malnutrition caused by a lack of protein. They had swollen legs and their hair had turned blond. They were dying.

"The war got worse. A local leader convinced her followers that they should cover their bodies in oil to protect themselves and that she had the power to turn stones into hand grenades. The rebels attacked our town four times.

"I was in the operating theater when the rebels attacked. First we heard shooting outside, then they came to the hospital. We hid under concrete tables until the fighting moved on. It wasn't a personal threat, it was just government and rebels.

"The fact that we were there and drove or walked about town was so good for the local people. Solidarity is underestimated. The fact that we were there when every other foreigner had left made people feel better."

Riekje had intended to go for half a year, but she stayed in Uganda for a year. From there she went on to Kenya, Mozambique, and Zambia. In all, Riekje has spent 17 years with MSF.

"Why? I believe in it. We contribute. We help. We were there when nobody else was there. When we ended the program in Kenya, the Somali chief said to me, 'Thank you very much. We can do it for ourselves now.'

"I am an idealist. I think if you have the capacity to do something for society, you should take up the challenge and do it."

ON MISSION IN CONGO

This is an excerpt from my journals when I was serving as MFS's head of mission in the Republic of Congo in 2004.

Arrivals and Departures

In the hurly-burly of immigration at Brazzaville's Maya Maya airport, four or five people checked my passport as I inched my way through the crowd. The spirit was more festive here than in some places in Africa, the people more gentle, and the machine guns not displayed so aggressively. From passport control, I shuffled to yellow fever control, where the woman in the booth looked disappointed to see that I had my card from Health Canada. I learned later that a sideline for the yellow fever control officials is selling cards to people who don't have them. So much for disease control.

I moved along with the crowd to the luggage reclaim, and then, out of nowhere, as I looked around the crowded, sweaty room and tried to guess where my bags might be, a slight and wiry man materialized beside me and said, "Monsieur David? Je suis avec Monsieur Paul. Je m'appelle Jean-Barnabé. Bienvenue á Brazzaville." I had arrived.

Ten days later, it was my turn to put on an MSF T-shirt and go with Jean-Barnabé to meet the newest arrival, Ute, a doctor from Germany. Jean-Barnabé had been a driver for the German embassy for 19 years, and lost his job when the Germans pulled out of Brazzaville because of the civil war. So he knows all about the airport, after years of picking up and dropping off foreigners.

There was a gaggle of people around the entrance to the arrivals. A loud, posturing, threatening guard pointed with his baton to an imaginary mark on the ground by my feet and said, "Why are you crossing this line? Back off! Back off!" I started to step back, but the instant the guard turned his back, Jean-Barnabé plucked at my sleeve and we scooted two steps forward to a corner. There we were confronted by another, larger, uniformed man brandishing his truncheon.

Jean-Barnabé can make himself invisible. He goes completely and utterly still, so passive that you lose sight of him in the moving throng. As soon as the truncheon-wielding guy looked away, Jean-Barnabé again grabbed my sleeve and we scuttled by him, too. We used this method to get as far as the yellow fever booth, and there we waited until a uniformed young man with a big smile asked, "Vous attendez le Colonel Qui?" Of course, we didn't know which colonel was arriving, so he shooed us good-naturedly back along the corridor. Jean-Barnabé's invisibility trick was no match for a colonel.

"I can always spot the MSF volunteers," Jean-Barnabé said as we stood watching a mix of Africans and Europeans coming off the Air France flight. "For two and a half years I've been doing this, and I can always … Look, there she is!" And of course he was right.

Two days later I was scheduled to fly to Nkayi with Ute and Daniel, a Congolese doctor trained in Cuba. Just as Jean-Barnabé does international flights, it is Luc who helps innocent foreigners through domestic flights. There is absolutely no way for an untutored Canadian to tell what is happening in that domestic check-in room. There are no signs, nothing to tell you what to do, just a packed throng of people all talking at once. We were booked on a TAC flight, yet everyone was swarming around the TAAG counter. Ute's ticket was for a flight two days ago and in someone else's name. But Luc knew what to do. Once he had worked his way up to, and then behind, the ticket counter, he looked back at the three of us on the edge of the crowd, smiled, and gave the thumbs up. But it was still another 20 minutes before he clambered back over for our bags.

When I left Nkayi a few days later it was early morning. The airport consisted of a red-clay airstrip with a little shed off to one side. I stood in the shed and watched a barefoot woman crossing the runway. The strap around her forehead went over her shoulders to hold a large basket on her back. Ignoring the passengers clambering down from the Aero-Service plane, she strolled with

The snack bar at Nkayi airport

great dignity across the runway and off to the sugar fields on the far side for another day's work.

We waited in the shed for quite a while. The plain around Nkayi is vast and flat with mountains in the distance. A solitary mango tree stands in front of the shed. The men wore handsome flowing robes—gold, red, green, silver. An old woman sat on the concrete floor, a dirty cloth spread on the ground before her with baguettes, bananas, and an open pack of cigarettes—this was the Nkayi airport snack bar. Off to one side stood an unstable metal table with the ticket agents for TAC and Aero-Service behind it. And again, mysterious transactions took place while I looked on in bewilderment.

The Aero-Service plane was painted, unlike the TAC plane that had brought me here, but the wavy red logo looked distressingly as though the tail of the plane was on fire. At the bottom of the steps into the plane, though, they had thoughtfully placed a boot scraper so we didn't track the sticky, clinging mud of Nkayi up into the cabin.

The interior of the old Russian plane was fancier than TAC's plane. For instance, the co-pilot didn't have to come back and pry open a ceiling panel over my head and reach into the exposed wiring to adjust a door-locking mechanism as he did on TAC. Signs in Russian and English warned: "No Smoking! Fast the Belts!"

On Friday I plan to cross the Congo River to Kinshasa in the Democratic Republic of Congo to visit our embassy there. Luc has already assured me he will get me on the boat safely, and has given me instructions about what to do on the other side. "You'll have to be careful," he advised me. "I hear it is disorganized over there.

Nkayi airport

MSF volunteer surveying the destruction of the tsunami in southeast Asia

CHAPTER 3

In Disasters and War Zones

The war was over. We made our way up the deserted highway and along a dirt track to the village where, we had been told, we would find hospital beds to bring back to the gutted remains of the district hospital we were rebuilding in Makeni.

We had been in this part of Sierra Leone a few weeks before, and our white land cruisers had frightened the villagers away—they remembered all too well that when people came to their villages in cars it was usually to kill, not to heal. This time, however, they recognized us, and we were welcomed by happy groups of running children.

We stopped outside the burned-out health clinic. As we waited for the chief, a toothless old man jogged over to a huge drum hanging in a tree and began beating it. Boom, boom, boom—the low sound rolled out over the land.

We went into the clinic. No beds there. The chief took us around the village, and gradually we found the beds—a pregnant woman was lying on one in this hut; in the next, a sick old man. These beds seemed to be the only furniture left in the entire village.

As we stood in the sun and discussed what to do, curious people emerged from the bush. They were responding to the call of the drum beat, wanting to see the guests who had come to this forgotten corner of Sierra Leone. They were curious. They were destitute. We could not take these beds. Even if the villagers had removed these beds from the burned-out clinic, how could we claim them for the hospital down in Makeni?

We made up our minds. We would find beds down in the capital—we would not take these beds. For the first time since we had arrived, the chief relaxed and a deep smile came over his face. And next time we came back, once the district hospital was working properly, we would bring nurses and doctors with us.

—DAVID MORLEY, 2002

THAT DAY IN 2002 when we went hunting for beds for the hospital in Makeni marked almost 20 years of MSF missions in Sierra Leone. The first mission was set up in 1986 to treat patients infected with cholera. In 1989 MSF volunteers cared for refugees who crossed the Sierra Leone border to escape the civil war in Liberia.

This 14-year-old girl lost her hands in the civil war in Sierra Leone. She and her son live in an MSF camp in Freetown.

In 1991 civil war began in Sierra Leone, and for the next 11 years, MSF's missions were in the middle of a war zone. The rebels of the Revolutionary United Front were ruthless in their assaults on civilians. More than 10,000 children were abducted and forced to become child soldiers; thousands of women were kidnapped, tortured, and raped. Rebels attacked innocent villagers with machetes, cutting off their ears, hands, and limbs. They looted and destroyed farms, homes, schools, and hospitals. While the war was raging, MSF volunteers worked in hospitals and in surgical tents treating the wounded and in camps where thousands of homeless people were given shelter, food, water, medical care, and a safe haven from the rebels.

The war was officially over in 2002, but the humanitarian crisis was not. It left the people of Sierra Leone without hospitals, doctors and nurses, and the most basic medical care. In its postwar missions, MSF began rebuilding hospitals and clinics and providing health services, while continuing to work in camps for refugees from Liberia and for the displaced people of Sierra Leone. MSF's work in Sierra Leone is one example of a long-term mission and the organization's commitment to helping the world's neediest people.

Setting Up a Mission

The hardest decision that people who work with MSF have to make is where to set up our missions. There are so many places where people need help. We know that our decision to serve in one desperate community means that another will go without.

When MSF hears about a violent conflict or a natural disaster, we send in an explo (exploratory) team. The members of the team assess how badly the situation has affected people's health, whether the country's health system can cope, and what other humanitarian organizations are involved. Then they report back to one of MSF's operational centers in Europe or North America.

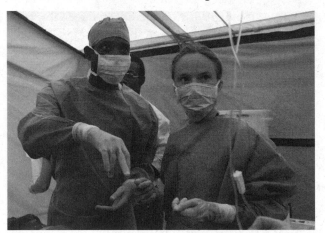

Tent surgery

The report from the explo team sets off discussions among volunteers that can go on for hours. But there are always limits to what we can do and where we can make the most difference, and sometimes the decision is more art than science. In the end, it comes down to helping people who have the greatest and most urgent needs.

Once the decision to set up a mission is made, it is up to members of the country teams to take action. How many doctors and nurses do we need? Do we need water and sanitation engineers? Is there risk of a cholera epidemic? Do people need food and shelter? How many national staff can we find quickly? Are the hospitals operating? How can we get to the people who need our help? When these questions have been answered, a request for volunteers goes out, medical kits are ordered, and transport is arranged.

In the case of a natural disaster, we can sometimes wind down a mission in a matter of months. When the crisis involves a civil war, it usually takes much, much longer. Many disease out-breaks—measles, ebola, meningitis—can be handled quickly. Others, like the big three killers—malaria, tuberculosis, AIDS—require long-term missions.

Ready-To-Go Emergency Kits

The more quickly MSF workers arrive on the scene, the more lives we can save. MSF is often the first humanitarian organization in the field because we have stockpiles of medical kits that are ready to go at a moment's notice. They include supplies for every kind of emergency—from a surgical hospital kit for treating 300 people a day to a basic mission kit that includes radios and land cruisers. The kits are designed to be mixed and matched to fit the needs of the mission.

MSF brings medical supplies to the hospital in Pristina, Kosovo.

Encouraging children to use latrines in Congo

Epidemics

There's always a risk of an epidemic—cholera, measles, yellow fever, or meningitis—when people are weak from hunger or injury and crowded together in places without clean water and latrines. When facing these conditions, the mission launches vaccination campaigns, constructs toilet facilities, and either digs new wells or fills huge bladders with trucked-in water.

An MSF volunteer fills huge bladders with clean, trucked-in water.

Complex Missions

Some of our most complex missions are in camps for refugees and people displaced within their own country by war or disaster. In these missions, we are usually dealing with more than one crisis: malnutrition; the risk of an epidemic; the lack of clean water and latrines; sometimes people with war wounds.

One of MSF's first jobs in a camp for refugees or displaced people is measuring their nutritional health. We are looking for acute malnutrition—people who are wasting away because they do not have enough food to eat.

MALNUTRITION FACTS

- People need 2,100 calories a day to stay healthy. Children and pregnant and nursing women need more.

- Children under the age of five are the first victims of malnutrition. They require small, frequent meals of nutritious food because they need the fuel of many calories in order to grow.

- Malnutrition kills because it lowers resistance to infections and viruses. Malnourished people often die from pneumonia, diarrhea, cholera, measles, malaria, and other diseases.

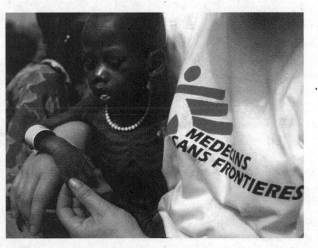

This child is suffering from marasmus, the most common form of acute malnutrition. Children with marasmus lose all fat and muscle and waste away because their families cannot feed them. Kwashiorkor is malnutrition that is caused by a lack of protein. Children with kwashiorkor have swollen bellies and faces.

Measuring Malnutrition

The MUAC (mid-upper arm circumference) bracelet is one of MSF's best tools for determining the nutritional health of young children. With the bracelet, we can screen a village or part of a refugee camp in a day or two. Since the effects of malnutrition show up rapidly in children who are under five years old, their malnutrition rate indicates the nutritional health of the whole community.

In Africa and parts of Asia, we often find up to 5 percent of young children with acute malnutrition. When the rate goes above 5 percent, we know that everyone is suffering. The MSF team gets to work immediately, setting up therapeutic feeding centers for malnourished children and making sure that the United Nations World Food Program is there distributing rations.

The MUAC bracelet is a color-coded measuring tape that is wrapped around the arm of a child who is between the age of six months and five years. If the circumference midway between a child's shoulder and elbow measures in the red zone—under 124 mm, the size of the small circle above— the child is suffering from severe acute malnutrition and is admitted to an MSF therapeutic feeding center.

Therapeutic Feeding Centers

When we find high levels of acute malnutrition, we set up our big white trigano tents to house a therapeutic feeding center. Nurses weigh and measure children under the age of five, because the relation of weight to height tells us if a child is eating enough food to grow.

When a child is admitted, we give her 8 to 10 very small feedings of a mixture made of milk, sugar, and oil. In the first few days—because her body systems are so weakened—we must restrict her food intake.

When a child starts to regain her appetite and respond to life around her, she is discharged from the 24-hour intensive care into the day care. Her amount of food is doubled, and she is moved into a supplemental feeding program until she is healthy and shows a normal weight for her height.

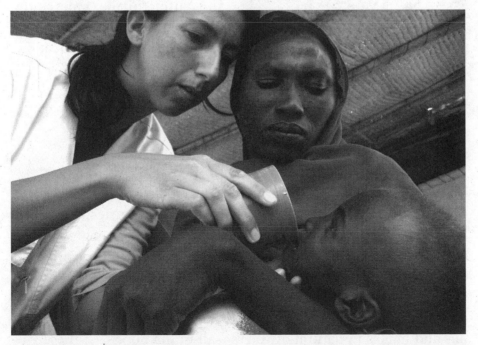

An MSF volunteer helps a mother and her child in a therapeutic feeding center in a camp for internally displaced people in Darfur, Sudan.

Caring for Mothers and Babies

In our missions in the world's poorest countries, MSF workers see pregnant women, mothers, and infants die at an alarming rate. In developed countries, the risk of a woman dying in pregnancy or childbirth is 1 in 2,800; in Africa, the rate skyrockets to 1 in 16. In the world's rich countries, the infant mortality rate is 5 deaths per 1,000 births. In sub-Saharan Africa, the rate is more than 20 times higher. Most of these deaths are due to poverty and the lack of basic health care.

MSF makes mother and infant care an essential part of our emergency and long-term missions. MSF sets up clinics where women can go for pregnancy check-ups, care before and after birth, emergency treatment, food, community support, and health education.

Mothers and babies wait outside an MSF clinic.

Mental Health Counseling

Many of the people MSF serves have been traumatized by death, destruction, and disaster. Often, their physical injuries heal much faster than their psychological and social wounds. Recognizing the need for counseling and support for victims of humanitarian crises, MSF began sending mental health workers into the field in 1991. They offer help to women who have been sexually abused, children who have been forced to kill, people who have lost families and homes in natural disasters—all in the hope that these victims can learn to cope with their horrors and rebuild their lives.

Treating Killer Diseases

Every 30 seconds, the world loses a child to malaria. Every year, tuberculosis claims 2 million lives; 350,000 people die from sleeping sickness; and another 2 million people are infected with kala azar. In Latin America, 15 million people are affected by Chagas disease. More than 90 percent of people who die from these diseases live in the world's poorest countries.

MSF runs malaria treatment programs in 40 countries; our expats and national staff have treated 1 million people since 1986. More than 60,000 people have been treated for sleeping sickness in Angola, Uganda, and Sudan. MSF has stepped up its treatment of tuberculosis to 32 projects running in 17 countries. But we know that fighting these diseases is not only about more programs and projects—what's needed to save more lives is effective and affordable drugs.

THE WORLD'S MOST NEGLECTED DISEASES

Malaria is a parasitic disease transmitted by infected mosquitoes in tropical climates, like sub-Saharan Africa.

Tuberculosis is a highly infectious disease passed from person to person by coughing or sneezing. More than 98 percent of TB deaths are in Africa.

Sleeping sickness is caused by the bite of an infected tsetse fly, which infests the water sources villagers use in 36 African countries.

Kala azar is a parasitic disease transmitted by sandflies that inhabit tropical forests, mostly in Bangladesh, India, Nepal, Sudan, and Brazil.

Chagas disease is transmitted by the vinchuca bug, which belongs to the same family as the tsetse fly but lives in 21 countries in Central and South America.

MSF calls malaria, tuberculosis, sleeping sickness, Chagas disease, and kala azar the world's most neglected diseases. They are neglected diseases because large pharmaceutical companies are not interested in developing and producing better drugs—they can't make big profits saving the lives of the world's poorest people. In 2003 MSF took action. It co-founded the Drugs for Neglected Diseases initiative, an independent, non-profit organization with a mission to work with scientists and researchers around the world to develop the drugs that will stop these diseases.

HIV/AIDS

MSF volunteers have been treating HIV/AIDS patients in its missions since the early 1990s, and they have watched the disease grow into a pandemic of enormous proportions with a staggering death toll—40 million people were living with the disease in 2005 and nearly 3 million died, most of them in sub-Saharan Africa.

But for MSF's national staff and ex-pats, the pandemic is not about numbers. It's about the people they see face-to-face every day—a 15-year-old girl dying of AIDS in Kenya; a 20-month-old Zambian boy infected by his mother at birth; a pregnant woman in South Africa infected by her husband; hospital beds in Uganda filled with AIDS patients dying from tuberculosis; and African grandmothers everywhere raising their children's orphans.

MSF is fighting HIV/AIDS in 27 countries with a "package of care" approach. Volunteers focus on testing for HIV/AIDS and treating patients, and also spread the word about prevention, distribute condoms, work with community groups, and support people with counseling.

MSF has been battling HIV/AIDS on a second front since winning the Nobel Peace Prize in 1999. That's when we began speaking out about the need for better and cheaper drugs to save more lives.

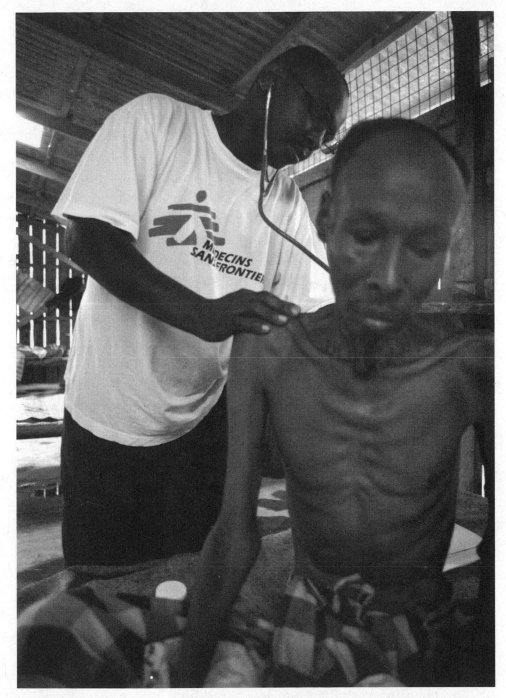

An MSF doctor in a clinic in Kenya examines a patient for suspected tuberculosis.

Campaign for Access to Essential Medicines

In the 1990s Christopher Ouma was a doctor at one of our clinics in Nairobi, the sprawling capital city of Kenya. One of his patients, a teacher at the neighborhood school, had AIDS, and Dr. Ouma was faced with a horrible dilemma.

"My patient contracted AIDS-related meningitis. The medication exists and could help him, but it costs $14 a day. After two weeks he had used up his savings and began selling his assets to pay for the medicine. At our clinic we had to advise him to stop selling his assets, and then we had to help him plan for his funeral. I'm a doctor. I want to treat patients, not plan funerals."

This story happens all over the world—17 million people die needlessly because they do not have access to essential medicines that could save their lives. Most of these people are the world's poorest, and they are suffering and dying not because the drugs to help them do not exist, but simply because they cannot afford to pay. The world's poorest people are not a lucrative market, so pharmaceutical companies have been in no rush to make live-saving drugs more affordable.

This immoral situation pushed MSF to create the Access to Essential Medicines campaign in 1999, using the money that came with the Nobel Peace Prize. This campaign moved us into the realm of business and politics, and we shifted some of our energy into boardrooms, government meetings, and public awareness in order to get the drugs we needed to save more lives.

Some people at MSF focused on convincing political and business leaders of the need to change patent laws so that cheaper AIDS medicines could be produced. Others developed grassroots awareness campaigns to alert people in rich countries about the fact that people in poor countries were dying because they could not afford life-saving treatment.

The brand-name pharmaceutical companies fought back, claiming that they had to charge high prices to earn enough to invest in new medicines and that it was simply impossible for them to lower their prices. But then in 2001, CIPLA, a drug company in India, started making and selling AIDS medicine at a fraction of the cost of the big pharmaceutical companies. Suddenly, the big drug companies changed their tune, and within months, the cost of AIDS medicine that had been selling for more than $10,000 per patient per year dropped to less than $1,000, and today the cost in many developing countries is as little as $140. Thanks to this low price, hundreds of thousands of people are alive today—working as productive members of society and caring for children who otherwise would have been orphans.

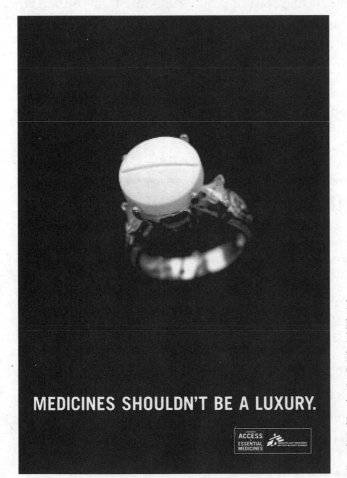

MEDICINES SHOULDN'T BE A LUXURY.

MSF mounted a public awareness campaign called Medicines Shouldn't Be a Luxury, and 40,000 Canadians sent postcards to then Prime Minister Jean Chrétien. In 2003, Canada became the first country to propose a law that would make it possible for low-cost generic medicines to be made in Canada and sent to poor countries, but by 2006 no medicines had been sent.

Telling the World …

On MSF missions in war zones, we are often the only outsiders in the midst of a dangerous civil conflict. We are providing life-saving medical care, but we are also a reminder to civilians that they have not been forgotten by the rest of the world, and that brings them hope. And sometimes—when we see horrific abuses against the people we are helping—we must tell the world about what we have witnessed.

How and when we should speak out is never an easy decision. It is one thing to remind guards at a military check-point that under International Humanitarian Law they must let impartial medical agencies like MSF have access to patients. Much more difficult is the decision to publicly denounce soldiers attacking civilians and committing terrible crimes that violate International Humanitarian Law. We are always aware of the risks of speaking out. When we denounce the atrocities of rebels or other warring parties in a conflict, they can deny us access to the people we are trying to help.

INTERNATIONAL HUMANITARIAN LAW

International Humanitarian Law (IHL) covers the rules of war. First agreed to in Geneva, Switzerland, in 1949 (and therefore also known as the Geneva Conventions), IHL is designed to protect people who are not part of the conflict and to restrict the means of warfare. In the heat of battle, these rules are often broken.

Some of the rules set out in IHL include:

- protection of all civilians, who must not be targets in war
- civilians must be allowed humanitarian assistance
- protection of humanitarian workers
- the use of force must not be more than needed

Sometimes we speak out to prod political leaders to end violence against our patients and innocent civilians. Sometimes we speak out to encourage other aid agencies to come and help us in a humanitarian crisis. Sometimes we speak out when we are concerned that the United Nations is not doing its job. But always we speak out because it is our responsibility as global citizens trying to save lives. We see things that many others do not, and so we must speak out.

About Chechnya

In 2000, MSF issued a report that exposed the horrible atrocities our volunteers were seeing on their missions in Chechnya—atrocities committed by the Russian military against the Chechen people. The report painted a picture of a place that had fallen into a state of terror and extreme violence.

With its report, MSF was asking Western governments to call the Russian army to account for its actions against Chechen civilians. But Western governments said nothing, and over the next 18 months two of our volunteers were kidnapped. Though they were eventually released, the message was clear—we could not send volunteers to help the beleaguered people of Chechnya. Our effort at speaking out had not worked.

About Darfur

The civil war raging in Darfur in western Sudan has been one of the most brutal in the twenty-first century. We first knew something was going on when our missions in Chad heard news of people crossing over the Sudan-Chad border by the tens of thousands.

Teams went on explo missions and came back to the capital with stories of horrific violence, of whole villages being burned, and of high levels of malnutrition among the children. We sent volunteers to the Chad-Sudan border in 2003, and soon we were the only providers of medical care for more than 200,000 refugees.

And nobody else came. Other aid agencies, which rely more

heavily on government funding than we do, couldn't start working until they got money from their governments. And other governments were not going to help because Darfur was not in the news.

So we contacted all the journalists we could and invited them to come to Chad—we still couldn't get into Darfur and the government of Sudan would not let our teams into the region. The journalists saw the horrible conditions of the refugees in Chad and heard the tragic stories of whole villages being destroyed, men and boys being killed, and women and girls being sexually assaulted. The journalists' reports finally touched public opinion, and governments began sending money to the United Nations and other aid agencies so they could help.

Increased international awareness also made it harder for the government of Sudan to keep aid agencies out of Darfur itself, and soon the people of the region were receiving assistance not only from our volunteers, but also from other humanitarian agencies. And having more international volunteers on the scene made it harder for the fighters to commit atrocities against civilians.

But the fighting continues. People are living in camps and do not feel they can safely go back to their villages. The limitations of our humanitarian work are made clear—we can help save lives, but the fighters and the people who are backing them must want the fighting to end for there to be a real peace for the people of Darfur.

Volunteers Around the World

These are just a few of the missions where MSF sent its volunteers in 2005.

Conflict Zones
Burundi
Colombia
Haiti
Somalia
Sudan

Camps for Refugees and Displaced People
Chad
Myanmar
Sierra Leone
Thailand
Uganda

Natural Disasters
India
Indonesia
Pakistan
Sri Lanka

HIV/AIDS Treatment
Armenia
China
Guatemala
Honduras
Niger
Peru
South Africa
Zambia
Zimbabwe

Diseases and Epidemics
Angola
Bolivia
Burkina Faso
Georgia
Guinea
Nigeria
Republic of Congo
Sierra Leone
Tanzania

Basic Health Care
Angola
Burundi
Ethiopia
Ivory Coast
Liberia
Republic of Congo
Russian Federation

WORKING TOGETHER

Sometimes we are the only agency in a humanitarian crisis; sometimes there are many. If we are the only one, we may find ourselves doing many more things than medical care—distributing plastic sheeting for shelters, setting up water systems, and distributing food. But usually other agencies turn up before too long.

In refugee camps, the United Nations High Commission for Refugees (UNHCR) is in charge of camp management, giving people the identity cards they need to receive food and supplies. Family reunification is a focus of the Red Cross. If CARE and OXFAM are present, they often work on water, sanitation, and housing. Child protection and education are covered by Save the Children.

Often, as crises continue, more agencies appear. Co-ordinating activities can take a lot of meetings as we see how well each agency works—and going to meetings is not something we like to do. When major disasters happen—the ones we hear about on CNN—it means that a lot of agencies are in the field, as there were after Hurricane Mitch in Central America and the tsunami in Asia. In these situations, we will often try to find another medical group to hand our work over to so we can free up volunteers and money to go to forgotten places where people are desperate and need our help.

ON MISSION IN BANGLADESH

Clea Kahn, an MSF volunteer from Toronto, served as project co-ordinator in the Nayapara refugee camp in Bangladesh in 2003. This is an excerpt from her journal.

Nayapara refugee camp has been the home of 13,500 Rohingya Muslims from Burma/Myanmar for more than 10 years. It's an absolutely horrible place, and I can't imagine living there for a week. People live cramped into tiny dwellings that swelter in the heat and leak in the rain. I recently visited a family of 12 living in four small, dripping rooms, with three blankets between them.

Most people exist on 10 liters of water per day, delivered at taps found around the camp, which are turned on for two hours in the morning and two hours in the evening. Every two weeks each family goes to collect their food ration: rice, lentils, oil, sugar, salt, and blended food (a powder made from soya, wheat, sugar, and added vitamins). Can you imagine living on this every

Nayapara refugee camp

63

day for 10 years? Once a month they get one bar of bathing soap per family, no matter how large the family is. That family of 12? One bar of soap to last the month.

On top of everything else, there's a lot of fear and tension. People are being repatriated to Myanmar and, from what we are hearing, quite a lot of them are afraid to go. We hear stories of people being harassed into "voluntarily" registering for repatriation. The UN High Commission for Refugees is supposed to be protecting them, but the UN people also want to close the camp, so they aren't as vigilant as they could be. We hear all the complaints about harassment and ill-treatment, because refugees come to us saying that they don't feel safe going into the UNHCR office. Taking down their concerns and passing them along is part of my job. While I'm not sure that my fist-pounding actually makes a difference (and I have to do it carefully, because MSF volunteers have been kicked out of the country in the past for being too vocal), it's a safe bet that it would be a lot worse if we weren't here.

Other parts of my job are more enjoyable, like spending time in our in- and out-patient departments and in our feeding centers. As the only non-medical team member, I don't get to save any lives, but I have managed to get some floors repaired, fix some beds that were wearing down, and make a few other small changes to help make life more bearable. I also drop by the food distribution center about once a week where we are monitoring to make sure that the refugees get their full ration. It's bizarre to have the whole operation grind to a halt so that I can inspect the quality of the rice (looks fine to me), check the lentils for insect infestation, or weigh a few bars of soap, but it does make a difference. Not only because I can then go bully the providers about the fact that bath soap is underweight by 10 grams, but also because it helps the morale of the refugees, who see some evidence that someone actually cares.

ON MISSION IN LIBERIA

Joe Belliveau, an MSF volunteer from Colorado, was a project coordinator in Liberia in 2003 during the civil war. This is an excerpt from one of his e-mails home.

MSF staff rush an injured child to a clinic after a rebel attack in Monrovia, Liberia, in 2003.

We approached slowly, duly cautious of young guys with drugs and guns.

We rolled down the windows and raised our sunglasses almost without thinking about it. The red and black MSF logo peppered our white vehicle and fluttered from our flag. We were among the first international visitors to this part of the country since the war escalated last March, but we knew they would recognize us as a humanitarian agency the instant we came into their sight. And all of us knew they were supposed to wave us on through their check-point, though in reality a few polite non-threatening words often speeds up the process.

"Hello, how de day? Could you open the gate for us, please?"

Normally, that would be sufficient, and a kid, AK-47 slung over his shoulder, would raise the bamboo bar or drop the string barrier. But now and then, especially if the drugs or cane juice were in full effect, they would be more bold and inquisitive.

"Wah you goh foh uh?" they said this time.

"Nothing, my friend, please open the gate."

But they would not give up so easily. Three of them walked up to our land cruiser and let their eyes wander across our cargo.

"We ah hungry," one of them said.

"Gentlemen, we are a medical organization on our way to carry out our work supporting clinics and hospitals. Now please lift the gate."

Two of them had had enough and wandered away, but the third, who couldn't have been more than 15 years old, was frustrated and fell into incomprehensible English with our driver. After a few moments of exchange, the young militia signaled his colleague to lift the gate and we were on our way.

"What did he want?" I asked Winston, our Liberian driver.

"He wanted us to help him find his mother."

Three weeks later, a teenage boy was transferred to the hospital we had only just begun supporting in northeastern Liberia. The boy had accidentally shot himself in the face. He had been sitting with his AK-47 pointed at the bottom of his chin and the trigger somehow went off. The bullet ripped through the bottom of his jaw, sliced through his cheek, and exited through his eye socket, taking most of the eye with it. There wasn't much we could do. We did not yet have surgical capacity, but we watched him closely and got to know him a bit.

Moses was a good kid, he was brave and intelligent, but still a boy. After a few days, he admitted he was 14 years old, not 24 as he had told us at first. We arranged for Moses to be transferred to Monrovia, the capital, where the Red Cross said they could do some basic surgery. Nothing like the plastic surgery that would make him look like himself again, but at least something to get him out of the life-threatening stage.

As the transfer day approached, Moses made a request. He had heard his family was in a refugee camp that was along the main road to Monrovia. Could we stop there on the way? He had not seen any of his family since April when a local militia group had forcefully recruited him along with any other fighting-age males they could find.

We were glad to help. It didn't take long to locate Moses's family since the United Nations refugee service had the camp organized quite well. Moses's sister was astonished and ecstatic, and when his mother saw him, she fell to her knees wailing.

Later that day, Moses arrived in Monrovia and was greeted by several of our local staff, including Winston who recognized Moses immediately as the check-point kid who had asked us to help find his mother. In a twisted kind of way, I guess we had.

ON MISSION IN MOZAMBIQUE

In 2000, I worked with MSF's logistical team in the aftermath of a devastating flood in Mozambique. This is an excerpt from my journals.

It is warm and dry now. The rains that destroyed so much of the Limpopo River floodplain seem a distant memory.

On the path in front of our tent, people go about their daily business. A small boy whistles as he tends a handful of goats and two big black cows. Women walk by with loads of wood for their fires.

Six weeks ago, almost nobody lived here in the village of Cheaquelane. But when the Limpopo River flooded its banks, people fled the valley looking for higher ground. The inhabitants of Chokwe came this far, 40 kilometers from home. Now 80,000 people live here in Cheaquelane.

When the first relief supplies arrived, a tent city was set up. It seems chaotic when you first come upon it, but in fact there is order to the chaos. For this is the whole city of Chokwe—teachers, nurses, religious leaders, farmers, and city officials—living in tents and shelters, and they have organized themselves as best they can. There is a bustling market, a big, green tent is city hall, and there are numerous church tents.

People rest in a camp in the village of Cheaquelane. Thousands were forced to flee from their homes when the Limpopo River flooded its banks.

In one corner of the camp, nestled under the shading branches of a stand of trees, is our therapeutic feeding center—four tents and a makeshift kitchen where the nutritional supplements are prepared. A team of doctors and nurses, both foreign and local, are doing what they can for the malnourished children of the camp.

Estela Perez, the medical co-ordinator, is a firebrand, laughing with the mothers, cajoling them, teaching them what they must do to bring their children back to health. In the little white tent that serves as the consulting room, each child is weighed, the charts are consulted, and instructions for the special diet they will need are given out. Estela gives full attention to each mother and child who comes to see her for a consultation.

"Look at you, you're getting chubby!" Estela turns to the mother and beams. "Well done, Mum, your baby is doing well."

Others are not so fortunate. "Oh dear, oh dear. I'm afraid this little one may leave us," she sighs. She turns to the child's mother. "Please, you must give her just this food for the next two days. No more than this." Then, quietly to herself, she mutters, "This place is deadly."

As night falls, the generator begins to purr. In the white tent, Estela and the medical team continue their consultations, while men string wires in the trees overhead and attach them to the generator and to lights in the tents so that nobody will trip over the sleeping children.

We sit in the lean-to kitchen and plan for tomorrow. In the nutrition center they are down to 8 severe cases out of the 70 children who still need to attend. "We do what we can with these ones," says Paula. "If they're strong enough, they'll make it. If not…"

Outside, the brilliant stars of the African night look close enough to touch. Singing starts in the camp, children's voices in those beautiful African harmonies, and the music and the drumming and the smell of wood smoke from cooking fires drift over the camp.

Tomorrow it will start again. More children will come to the center. Away in Chokwe the reconstruction will continue, and hopefully, the people in the camp at Cheaquelane will be one day closer to going home.

PART 2

Journals from the Field

ON ALL MY MISSIONS with MSF, I would crack open my journal at the end of each day and write about how our work was going, how our patients were doing, what we were seeing, and how it felt.

The next three chapters are excerpts from my journals—from El Salvador, where I was assessing an emergency preparedness project in the aftermath of an earthquake; from Congo in 2004, when I was responsible for advocacy activities as the civil war wound down; and from Zambia, where I was assessing an HIV/AIDS project in one of the remotest parts of the country.

Pequeña Inglaterra, El Salvador

CHAPTER 4

Earthquake in El Salvador

El Salvador, After the Earthquake

25 January 2001

In the morning the team meets in the MSF house in San Salvador. The teams have come from around Central America, volunteers who were working on AIDS projects in Guatemala, water projects in Honduras, in the Emergency Preparedness Office in Costa Rica, and the people who have come here for this emergency. They plan the day's activities: who will go to Armenia—one of the hardest hit towns—to support the building of a little cholera center in the hospital there; who will go to Cafetalon to continue our mental health and water programs for the 7,000 people from Santa Tecla and neighboring towns, who are living in the football field and who, unless things change, will be there for quite a while yet.

Vincent Brown, who has come here from Epicentre, the MSF research center in Paris, briefs us on the data he has collected on diarrhea and respiratory problems in the country, and how these figures should help the team plan the next steps.

Then we are off to Armenia. Armenia is just 40 minutes from San Salvador, but it could be on another planet. The busy boulevards of San Salvador, with their McDonald's and Pizza Huts and car dealerships, look like any other bustling Latin American capital. Armenia, before the earthquake, would have looked like a provincial Latin American town. The central square dominated by its church, one-storey buildings made of brick and adobe. A sleepy place.

Now it looks like the aftermath of an aerial bombardment. There is rubble everywhere in the streets. In every block of houses one is gone, replaced by a pile of bricks, mortar, wood, and tin. Occasionally you can see broken pieces of tables and beds. You would never guess that these piles could ever have been homes full of life. They look like they have always been this way, just useless rubble. For street after street after street, the destruction goes on.

The destruction is even worse than it first appears. Many of the fronts of houses are still standing, but behind them there is nothing but rubble. Many people are sleeping in the streets, underneath makeshift plastic roofs. It will take 2 million sheets of zinc to provide the most rudimentary reconstruction. The largest manufacturer here in El Salvador produces 100,000 per year. How long will it be before these people have homes again?

A bookcase peeps out of one little green plastic tent in front of a pile of rubble—a student must live there. Down another street a group of mourners sit around a coffin. They are bathed in a blue light cast by the plastic sheeting that has been strung above them as an awning. An elderly man tosses great chunks of stone from the wreck of his house into the street, while his grandson diligently works beside him trying to rebuild his tricycle. And everywhere you see beautiful red, purple, and white blooms of bougainvillea looking impassively over the rubble surrounding them. I cannot imagine the power that it must have taken to wreak such havoc, to turn so many homes into nothing.

Some people are living in makeshift camps. MSF provides the water in San Martin. "Everyone pitched in," says Claudine, an MSF volunteer from Belgium. "We shared the work in this camp with UNICEF and Action Contre le Faim."

In the middle of town, MSF is supporting the work of the local clinic. We will use a garage to build a little center to treat diarrhea. Pierre, a French engineer who drove supplies here from the MSF emergency stockpiles in Honduras, works with the Salvadoran health staff figuring out how the center will look. "We'll use plastic sheeting to make the walls and divisions for the men and women. We have to make channels for the water so it doesn't contaminate that cistern over there. We need to string 2 by 4s there so we can hang the rehydration IV bags." They draw rough plans in their notebooks. "Do we have the cement we need to make the channels?" someone asks. "It's in San Salvador, we can bring it tomorrow morning and we'll be done by Saturday," Pierre answers.

A health official comes up and asks Claudine if we can help them do a fumigation of areas at risk of dengue fever. "We did a dengue campaign here in the fall, we have trained some local health promoters. It's good to see that they have seen the signs and are taking the initiative to come to us for help."

Then we go to Santa Tecla. This is the community that was hit with the mudslide, the town whose suffering has been on TV screens around the world. The victims are living in a football field. "When we arrived last Monday," says Pierre, "everyone was living in makeshift huts. We got the water system running with the tanks and the plumbing supplies we brought from Honduras, and the Red Cross brought in some tents. This is the kind of place where, if you don't get the sanitation down fast, cholera can kill before you know it."

In two days a cholera center was built on a basketball court beside the soccer field, with all the different sanitation zones, drainage, water supply, and tents. Latrines and washing stations were built at different places around the football field—which is now home for more than 7,000 people. MSF built a hut and distributes oral rehydration solution and we are also running a mental health program to try and help people deal with the psychological trauma of this catastrophe.

So far, there is only one suspected case of cholera. "If we are really lucky," says Pierre, looking around the empty cholera center, "we will never have to use this place. We moved fast here, and maybe there won't be a cholera outbreak. But in 1986, last time there was an earthquake here in El Salvador, some people had to live in tents like this for six months, so it is good that we've built this well. If it doesn't have to be used for cholera, we will find another use for it. It could be used as a school or a community center."

The great thing is that almost all of this material is reuseable. The tents, the plastic sheeting, a lot of the wood—when this crisis is finished we will store it all again and be ready for when the next emergency hits.

"Basic hygiene is so important," Pierre says. "In our emergency kits we include soap, towels, washing up things, plates, and utensils. These help keep people healthy."

At the end of the day, people come back to the MSF office in San Salvador. It has been a hot day, and everyone is sticky and dusty. In one room, the water and sanitation people work on the design for a latrine. In another, people pour over health statistics from another community and ponder if we can help there, too. The mental health team sits quietly together, debriefing after the day's work. The sun has set, and the temperature is cooling off.

+ + +

The road to hell leads to Comasagua. Nothing I have ever seen has prepared me for what I saw there.

You go up into the mountains where the earth shook so hard that the steep mountain walls came tumbling down—huge boulders, trees, telephone poles—they all crashed with unimaginable force into the humble homes of the people whose only place to live was up on those precarious slopes. It is 15 kilometers of endless destruction, and nobody will ever know how many people lie buried beneath the landslides.

For mile after mile you drive in swirls of dust. Our talk of medical programs and plans grows silent as we look at the destruction around us. Bits of broken houses—crushed tin roofs, scraps of cardboard, wooden support poles, beds, children's clothing, dishes, a broken chair—line the road. At one perilous curve along the mountainside, a huge mound of earth covered and destroyed 13 houses. It seems impossible that just two weeks ago homes were here and people went about their ordinary lives. Now it looks like a massive open-pit mine.

There is no color; brown dust covers everything. The bougainvilleas are brown. The leaves on the trees are brown. You walk on the road and you sink into the dust. It's like walking across a field of freshly fallen brown snow—except the dust gets into everything, your hair, your eyes, your clothes. Your footprints show where you have walked. They look like the footprints the astronauts left behind on the moon.

But we are not on the moon. We are here on earth. In fact, Comasagua is closer to my home in Toronto than are many parts of Canada. We are not far away at all.

About 12,000 people live in Comasagua. And 9,000 of them lost their homes in the earthquake. The survivors live in the streets, in small shelters of wood and plastic sheeting. Some camps are being built on the few flat spaces around the town—one is on a coffee farm on the edge of town, another on a football field. But the people of Comasagua are not sure if they want to move to these camps—they want to stay as close as possible to all that remains of their homes, even though walls lean drunkenly out over streets that are filled with rubble. Both churches, the town hall, and the health center were all destroyed.

We will set up a tent in front of the ruined clinic where our doctors and nurses can see patients. "We are an optimistic people," a Salvadoran colleague tells me. They will need all their optimism and strength to cope with the destruction of this earthquake.

Comasagua Revisited

Eighteen months ago, just days after the earthquake here in El Salvador, I was in Comasagua, a shattered town of broken houses covered in dirt. It was horrific—swirling dust, piles of rubble that had been homes just days before, dishes scattered about. A fine brown dust covered everything. Survivors were listless with shock and grief.

Today, I got to go back, and saw a rebirth—this small Salvadoran town is alive once more. The bougainvilleas are in bloom, but this time they are brilliant purple and red on a background of deep green leaves—not sad, brown, dust-covered plants.

The central square of Comasagua is no longer home to the survivors of the earthquake living in tin shanties. Now it is an ordinary square once again, just like any little Central American town. The huge piles of rubble are gone, and the town's churches have been rebuilt. The little market has been rebuilt, too, and painted a bright orange. The Health Post is up and running. On the edge of town survivors live in neat new houses built for the people whose homes were destroyed.

This is a miraculous transformation—and we were a part of it, supporting health delivery in a tent in the local schoolyard until the Health Post was rebuilt; building latrines to make sure that disease could not spread; developing systems to catch and use rainwater so that people could have pure water to drink; training local health workers on how to respond during the emergency before the reconstruction was complete.

I suppose I shouldn't call it miraculous, because the key elements were the hard work and perseverance by the people of Comasagua. But we were able to help in the reconstruction here—and it worked.

Pequeña Inglaterra

More than 5,000 people around Santa Tecla lost their homes in last year's earthquake. At first, they lived in temporary shelters in a soccer field where we provided water, mental health support, and built a field medical center. I suspect the authorities didn't know where they would find all these people permanent homes, so when a man from England donated some land for houses that problem was solved.

Well, not entirely, because they still had to build the houses. There were difficulties, and at first the people had only temporary homes—"microwave ovens" our Country Manager called them—just a little tin structure that bakes its inhabitants in the tropical sun. But the government and Plan International are now providing material so people can build cement-block homes. We are working in health, water, and sanitation. We have helped provide latrines and are working on water disposal. Using simple technology, we have made wells that provide good drinking water. On a grassy hill under a huge shade tree, we built a simple Health Post and are meeting with local officials to make sure that the people of Pequeña Inglaterra (Little England) get access to the nearby government clinic.

Standing beside the Health Post, I look out at Pequeña Inglaterra. Down one lane I see one of our volunteers putting the finishing touches on a well. Behind me I hear Flor, our nurse, training people in the use of dry latrines. Everywhere I look I see men, women, and children building their homes. The sound of hammers fills the air. Before my eyes a new community is being born.

I remember when I was here last year one of our staff said to me, "We Salvadorans are an optimistic people." At the time I thought that there was no reason for optimism, no reason for hope in the aftermath of that terrible earthquake. Well, I was wrong, very wrong. That optimism was more than justified.

Cement-block homes being built in Pequeña Inglaterra

CHAPTER 5

Civil War in Congo

The Unknown Country

25 January 2004

His yellow eyes have trouble focusing and the lollipop lolls in the corner of his mouth. He is stoned, about 17 years old, and the necklace made of purple thread and the machine gun slung over his back identify him as a Ninja fighter at this check-point on the road between Brazzaville and Kinkala in Pool Province in Republic of Congo.

Republic of Congo, the other Congo, sits on the north shore of the Congo River, across from the much larger and more infamous Democratic Republic of Congo (DRC). Like its neighbor to the south, Republic of Congo has been devastated by civil wars and unrest for the past decade. Unlike DRC, Congo rarely makes the headlines in the West, although these wars have been a humanitarian catastrophe for the average Congolese. This fertile country, once considered one of the most developed in sub-Saharan Africa, is in ruins.

Ninja fighters in Congo

Pool has been the main battleground and the people of Pool, the main targets of the war. The president of Congo, Denis Sassou-Nguesso, comes from the north of the country. Pool Province, in the south, is the most heavily populated and fertile part of the country, and home to the main political opposition. The wars started after elections in 1992 when the vote split along ethnic lines and Mr. Sassou-Nguesso lost power. Different armed factions—Ninjas, Cobras, Cocoyes—fought throughout the country. But in Pool and Brazzaville, the war became one of ethnic punishment, with devastating humanitarian results. By the end of that year, the United Nations estimated that more than one-quarter of Congo's population had been forced to flee their homes, and that one-third of the displaced women had been raped.

For 12 months during 2002-2003, the army sealed off Pool from the outside world, and both sides engaged in military activities that resulted in another surge of internally displaced people and the destruction of homes, hospitals, churches, and schools. A truce was signed in 2003, but neither the government nor the opposition Ninjas have been able to agree on a plan to disarm and reintegrate the fighters. Check-points remain throughout the province, and extortion by men with guns remains the norm for people who risk a trip on the roads.

In the spring of 2003, a medical team from MSF was finally able to enter Pool. The health status of the survivors was deplorable, with high levels of malnutrition. Many towns and villages have less than half the number of inhabitants they had when the wars began. People fled to the forest and spent a year in hiding—and the survivors have straggled back to find their villages destroyed. Health centers and schools were targeted during the fighting. Teachers, doctors, and nurses fled, and now only some have returned. Years of violence, extortion, pillaging, and rape have broken traditional social structures, and MSF teams find old people left with no one to care for them, families scattered, and women and children on their own. The survivors of this conflict have endured unbearable suffering and are still living in uncertainty and fear. People have seen family members killed and raped.

"This is a lost generation," says an MSF nurse once the yellow-eyed Ninja has let us pass. "Schools haven't been open for seven years, and when little kids see their big brothers with guns slung over their shoulders, they think that's what they want to do when they grow up. And without any real peace process, how will the Ninjas disarm? I was stopped by one up in Yangui who said to me 'How can I give up my gun? Where would I go? If I go to my village they don't want to see me—they know I'm a Ninja. And if I go to Brazzaville I'm dead meat.'"

Out and out fighting may have stopped, but life holds little security for the people of Pool. The schools stay shut, the only free medical service is provided by international agencies, the stalemate continues, the check-points stay up, the United Nations presence stays small. This is the reality here in the other Congo, the Congo the world has forgotten.

Making It Work

So what is MSF working on here in Congo?

We have six different projects around the country. They are in two very different contexts, so different that sometimes it is hard to believe we are in the same country at all.

In Nkayi and Mossaka, we are treating sleeping sickness. We send out screening teams—in Nkayi by land cruiser and Mossaka by boat—to test people and then send those who are positive to a treatment center. In Kellé, up in the land of the deadly ebola virus, we are training people on how to treat ebola. The other three projects are basic health care missions. They are all in Pool—Kinkala, Kindamba, and on the edge of Brazzaville.

Here in the office in Brazzaville is where everything is co-ordinated. Since almost nothing is made locally, this is a big logistical project, and the logistics center downstairs bustles during the

A mobile clinic in Loulombo

week. Nawel does the international medical ordering (and when ex-pats arrive with a few thousand vaccines she always does a little jig for joy); Fred co-ordinates all the movement and the building rehabilitation. With such a terrible infrastructure in Congo, and with projects that use boats as well as land cruisers and the uni-mog, there is a lot of co-ordination. Fred reminds me of a stage manager in a play, as he figures out the movements—if Jupiter (our big unimog truck that can go just about anywhere) is here, and we need to get supplies and an ex-pat there, and Coco (one of the land cruisers) is having trouble with its four-wheel drive, how will he get the malaria parachecks to Kindamba by Wednesday? Fred figures out how to make it all happen.

The radio is key for communicating and for knowing where everyone and everything is at any one time. In Pool we have a self-imposed curfew of 6:00 p.m. so we keep track of the vehicles on mobile clinics to make sure they leave the villages in time to get back. The radio room is filled with maps and charts of distances between places, and places where we must call in, and where check-points and difficult river crossings are. A few weeks ago one of the land cruisers got stuck in a swamp and we had to abandon it for the night—it was fine when we got back. And for security in Pool, we always travel with two vehicles, so it is a big operation.

The radio chatters away all day, and radio jargon and static are constantly in the background. Each project base has its own name. It started with the radio operator's alphabet (Alpha, Bravo, Charlie, Delta), so we are Hotel Bravo here; Nkayi is Hotel November; Mossaka, Hotel Mosquito; and Kinkala, Hotel Kilo. But as the mission grew and we got more bases that began with K, we improvised with Hotel Kingston for Kindamba and, everyone's favourite, Hotel California for Kellé.

The warehouse next to the office is made of a few old cargo containers, and we have another one 10 minutes away. We also keep emergency supplies in both the MSF house and the MSF office in case the war starts up again and we would need to treat people here in town. And we have generators and back-up systems and coolers to make sure the cold chain—our system of keeping vaccines and other medicines at the right temperature—remains intact.

It is a well-run operation, and it works. This is MSF's behind-the-scenes action that makes it possible for us to give medical assistance to the people who need our help.

Kinkala

26–28 January

We left Brazzaville in Jupiter and Shaetan. Jupiter is a great big truck, high off the ground. Shaetan is a four-by-four land cruiser. We drove out along the wide avenues of Brazzaville, our MSF flag blowing in the wind. Green taxis and fancy private cars were replaced by public transport mini-buses as we reached Bacongo and Makelekele. This area was deserted in March at the end of the most recent war. Now it is bustling. A good sign.

Out in the country the green fertile hills roll into the distance. Highway 1 is the road we are on and many places are impassable and we have to go off road. Twice we got stuck in Shaetan, and Jupiter had to pull us out. In 1985 this trip took a little over an hour. Now it takes six hours to go 60 kilometers. The government just let the road weather away—in places the crevasses are 30 meters wide. Along the road we passed military check-points, then Ninja check-points. Finally, we reached Kinkala.

The MSF house is at one end of town. The road winds up by the provincial administrative buildings—one-storey buildings arranged around a square. The prefect's office has been freshly painted, but other buildings have lost their roofs and have trees growing through the entrance ways.

Across the street is the district hospital in a series of low buildings—maternity, epidemics, out-patient, surgery, TB. When we started here last spring, there were startling numbers of malnourished children, and we set up a therapeutic feeding center (TFC). But the numbers have declined to a level where we could close the TFC and are running a mobile clinic to five or six outlying villages. Iain, an MSF doctor from Scotland, and Elke, a doctor from Germany, are doing a wonderful job in difficult circumstances. As we prepared for a meeting with the hospital administration, Iain and Elke had to leave. A woman had carried her 16-year-old son on her back from Matoumba, many kilometers away. He was having trouble breathing, and his neck was badly swollen. Iain and Elke were gone for the rest of the day. That night, Iain pored over a huge book of tropical medicine and finally found what was ailing the boy. An obscure disease made worse by malnutrition and parasites. "Are there any open-heart facilities in Brazzaville?" he asked no one in particular, knowing that the answer was no. He quietly closed his book. "That wee lad won't live."

Stuck on Highway 1 between Brazzaville and Kinkala

Bush Surgery in Kindamba

1 February

Kindamba is in the north of Pool, in the heart of Ninja country. Before the war Kindamba had 20,000 people. Today it has 3,000. Many houses are falling down; others are covered with Ninja graffiti.

MSF provides the health services for Kindamba, and we have some mobile clinics. Poor roads make the mobile clinics difficult, and check-points with stoned Ninjas don't make it any easier. Sometimes we have to spend six hours travel for three hours of clinic. Over lunch I talked with Marissa, our volunteer midwife from Kenya, who believes that we should put more effort into working with local health committees and start up or revive village clinics. They would do better. But the trouble is that we are still in the midst of conflict. In some places we tried supplying clinics, but some warring gang with guns would inevitably loot them.

When we started working here in October, the main health problem was malnutrition. People had been hiding in the bush, and they were starving. We set up a therapeutic feeding center in the hospital and sometimes it had 50 children at a time. That acute phase has passed, and we have been able to close the TFC and the remaining malnourished children have been admitted to the hospital.

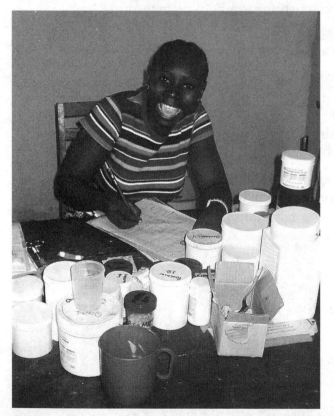

A member of our Congo team checks drug supplies.

We have in-patient services, and the most common ailment is malaria. ACT, the artemisinin-based combination therapy we are using, "is just incredible," says Simon, an MSF doctor. "In just three days it works! You bring them in for overnight so you can see them take the first two doses, and then you can be pretty sure they will take the final dose at home."

We also run a maternity ward and a mother-and-child center in the hospital in Kindamba. Last week, a woman went into labor, and when Simon, Steve (another MSF doctor), and Marissa reached the hospital, they could see this difficult labor might end in the death of both mother and child.

"We decided we would have to try a symphysiotomy—a surgical procedure to widen the pelvis—or else the baby and mother would die," said Simon. "We just don't see this being done in the West. In these situations, we do caesareans, but in Kindamba in the middle of the night we had to do what we could."

Outside, the sky was filled with thunder and lightning. Inside, Simon, Steve, and Marissa got to work. They had only a solar panel lamp and a miner's headlight to see by. They had the MSF guidelines on how to do symphysiotomies with them, and using it as a guide, Simon started the procedure, while Steve cleared away the blood. The mother was only under local anesthetic, and was calling, "Maman, Maman." The baby was pushing, blood was everywhere, then suddenly—whoosh—the baby was born into Marissa's waiting arms. "The baby had only the tiniest little nick above her ear," Simon marveled later, "and I had all my fingers left, too."

Mother and baby are doing well after bush surgery in Kindamba.

The Weevils

9 February

Well, they are flour beetles actually, the man at the University of Greenwich told me when I explained the situation to him via e-mail. But I still think of them as weevils. But no matter, because when we received stale-dated, weevil-infested sacks of Corn Soya Blend (CSB) for our patients, that just wasn't good enough. So I contacted the food technologist in the UK who said that the stale-date could be overlooked until the end of March. But we still had the problem of the weevils.

I first met the weevils last week in Nkayi. Our logistician, Mario, had found them in our most recent food shipment. He took me into our storeroom, and through a hole in one of the bags marked "Corn Soya Blend/World Food Program/A Gift from the People of Germany," he dug out bits of weevil-infested food with a spoon and put the sample in a ziplock bag, which I then brought back with me to Brazzaville.

Yesterday, as the weevils happily munched away, I counted them and discovered that the infestation rate of the sample was 2.5 weevils per cc. I had a meeting this morning with officials from the UN's World Food Program. I took the clear plastic bag of weevils with me, but the shy little critters hid in the CSB, so when I pulled the bag out and placed it on the gleaming table in the tidy office, the dramatic effect was lost. But the officials did agree that they should review their fumigation process.

More interesting was the reaction in the MSF office. Upon seeing my bag of weevils, one ex-pat who had been on multiple missions said dismissively, "Pfft! That's not a real infestation." But I agreed with what Mario, on his first mission, had said back in Nkayi. "I wouldn't want to eat this. Our patients don't want to eat this. In Canada, Public Health would close down a supermarket that sold infested flour. It is just unacceptable!" In the meantime, the weevils scurry around in their bag on my desk, and I have offered a prize to the person who can guess how many I have.

Sleeping Sickness in Nkayi

11 February

Here in Nkayi we are focusing on sleeping sickness. It is caused by the bite of the tsetse fly—most victims are villagers bitten while working in the fields. There was a national sleeping sickness program in Congo, but as with just about everything else here, it crumbled during the war and the infection rate soared.

We send out screening teams to do a simple test to see if the disease is present, and in smaller outlying villages, we also do some basic health care. In Cuvette we do this by boat along the Congo River and its tributaries. In Bouenza we do it by land cruiser. The teams go out for a couple of weeks at a time; health educators go a day ahead to villages and are followed by nurses and lab technicians who do the tests. When we have enough cases, they are sent to Nkayi or Madingou, where we have in-patient facilities within national hospitals.

The beds are in dimly lit 10-bed wards, and each bed has its own colorful mosquito net tucked above it for the day. Each patient must bring a caregiver to help, usually a family member

The hospital in Nyayi where MSF ran a sleeping sickness program

who knows the patient well enough to help with the physical care and who can tell us if the symptoms are changing. As we go on rounds Sara, a British doctor, and Daniel, a Congolese doctor, go through each patient's history, while a goat bleats at the end of its tether in the hospital courtyard.

The sleeping sickness parasite can lie dormant for a long time, or it can move quickly. Really, we don't know a lot about this disease—although we do know that if it is not treated it will kill everyone who has it. People's moods change. They can grow irritable and appear insane; they start sleeping and sleeping until they lapse into a coma.

This is a big, complicated type of project. It requires transporting screening teams into the bush. It requires medical support and good labs. And it requires medicine.

The medicine accepted as the official treatment by the Ministry of Health here is melarsaprol, an arsenic-based drug that requires months of intravenous treatment. And one of the side effects is death—it kills some patients. "You see patients cringing as the melarsaprol goes up their arms and into their bodies," Sarwat, our medical co-ordinator from Yemen, told me. "They are so brave, but after they have been getting this course of treatment, it corrodes their veins. If they are released and they come back in for treatment after three or four months, you still cannot find their veins." This is one of the tragedies we face—bringing in patients whose blood count told us they were going to get sleeping sickness, treating them with melarsaprol, and then watching them die from the drug.

There is another drug, DFMO, that does not have death as a side effect. But it is more complex to administer and requires a longer hospital stay. MSF is involved in a study using DFMO in combination with another drug to reduce treatment time—since patients must pay for every day they stay in the hospital. The problem is that the old, deadly medicine is cheaper than DFMO, and governments in places like Congo make decisions based on the bottom line. At one of our meetings with the Ministry of Health here, Sarwat challenged a senior official: "If your child were sick, would you give him melarsaprol or DFMO?" He refused to answer—and melarsaprol is still the official Congolese treatment for sleeping sickness.

Measles!

22 February

I got an e-mail from Claudette and André, our volunteers in Kellé, up in the north of the country. They have heard rumors of a measles outbreak in a town called Etoumbi, about two hours away.

I have sat in countless Canadian classrooms saying to kids, "What is the world's biggest preventable killer of children under five?" They rarely get the answer right. It is measles.

A severe case of measles

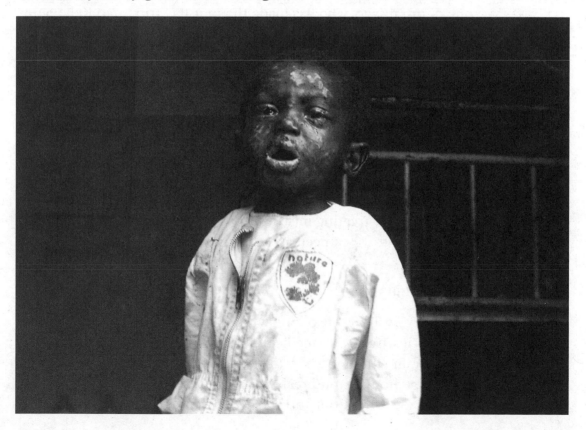

I sat down to do some planning with Dr. Ocean, our Congolese doctor, and Nawel, our very experienced logistician from Belgium. First, we needed to see if the rumors were true or not. Ocean will contact his colleagues at UNICEF (United Nations International Children's Emergency Fund), and see if they have heard anything about a measles outbreak.

As the radio operator tracks the movements of some vehicles in Pool doing a mobile clinic, Nawel and I sit in the hot, crowded radio room figuring out what needs to be done. We will need our two volunteers in Kellé to find out if there really is a measles outbreak, how it compares with previous outbreaks, if the Ministry of Health has the capacity to treat an outbreak, and if the ministry has vaccinated people in the area—or if it has just pretended to in order to get some money from donors for having good vaccination figures. Gilbert, one of our drivers who has made the four-day trip up to Kellé, joins us and goes over the road problems around that area.

I e-mail instructions to Claudette and André, and ask them to let me know if they can do this. Nawel reminds me not to be too Canadian. "You guys are always asking people if they want to do such and such. Be sure to tell them what to do, not ask!"

Back to my office, where I try to calm down from the adrenaline rush. We have a few thousand vaccines coming into the country with a new volunteer who arrives in a couple of days. Nawel and Sarwat have made sure we have the supplies here in Brazzaville for treating measles, so if the Ministry of Health needs some support we can get the stuff up there on the next flight.

24 February

Yesterday I was on the phone with MSF's office in Amsterdam, getting advice from our medical staff there about what we should look for in situations like this, and what medical complications may arise from an outbreak of measles. They were ready, in case this rumor turned out to be true, to provide us with emergency support for treating or vaccinating people, and we discussed shifting some medical staff away from some other projects to go up to Kellé.

Then last night I received the report from André and Claudette. It had taken them nearly four hours to get from Kellé to Etoumbi, but at least when they got there the news wasn't as bad as we had feared. There were 14 cases of measles in the first week of February, then 2 cases last week, and 3 more this week—so it looks as though the worst is over. Claudette, a nurse from Quebec who is suffering from malaria, felt that the health center in Etoumbi has things under control.

But get this! Sixteen of the 19 cases were children who had been vaccinated for measles. What does that say about the Congo's national vaccination campaign? Fortunately, none of the children in the Etoumbi outbreak has died. And it doesn't look as if we will have to arrange a measles vaccination campaign. While the volunteers here are glad for the people, there was also a bit of a letdown, since people wanted to get out of the capital and into the bush to do some hands-on work.

Congo Health Care

1 March

I find the health system here extremely frustrating. In the 1980s, some African states instituted a system called cost-sharing, in which the patients would contribute 15-20 percent towards the cost of health services and the state would maintain hospitals and clinics and cover the costs of medicines and supplies.

It hasn't worked out that way. Cost-sharing is covering only about 5 percent of the costs of health services. And in places where there are no checks and balances, where there are wars, and where the poor are not educated, the opportunities for abuses are endless.

In Nkayi, I talked with Dieudonné, the guy who runs the local vaccination program. He gave me all the right answers, but his eyes shifted when he spoke. "In principle, yes," he answered very precisely and carefully when I asked him if vaccinations in Congo are free. The bottom line? The people of Congo have to pay a dollar for a vaccination card—although he told me that people can buy a cheaper card in the market down the street for just a quarter. And, yes, kerosene for the cold chain can also be a problem that patients need to help out with. And then those syringes, well, they're another 50 cents. It may not sound like much, but we have to remember that the per capita income here is just $2.50 a day.

"Look, if we gave away the cards for free," Dieudonné continued, "how would those people who sell the cards make a living?" Dieudonné also admitted that mothers who cannot afford the cards do not have their children vaccinated, which puts their children at greater risk for measles, polio, or other easily preventable childhood diseases. Once again, it is the poor who suffer the most.

Iain caring for a child in Kinkala

Congo Farewell

3 March

I have been writing about the problems here so much that I fear I have given friends at home a skewed picture of this place. The dawn chorus of morning songbirds; the man who climbed up the mango tree outside my window with a basket on a pole to harvest the fruit; the fishermen on the Congo River, polling upstream in their dugout canoes; the boys swimming in the Congo and clambering up unseen to stow away on the Brazzaville-Kinshasa ferry; the family who lives in a cargo container and planted a flower garden out front; the beautifully colored cloth worn by both women and men, and the dignity of their bearing as well—these are all Congo, too.

I think of sitting after work chatting and laughing with colleagues about African soccer and hearing about the villages in Bouenza, in Sangha, in Cuvette, and in Pool, which are the homes of our national staff. These are friendly and helpful and welcoming people. I am impressed by them all—and not just because of their extraordinary commitment to our work. I am particularly impressed because on our staff we have men and women both from Pool and from the north. Northerners and southerners have been killing each other in this civil war, and yet our staff here are able to work together. It is not always easy, but these people who have been taught to hate each other do an absolutely amazing job of working together.

I briefed two new volunteers this morning—Arjan who is going to Pool and Marina who is on her way to Nkayi. As we were talking, Dr. Ocean came in. He smiled, but his eyes were sad, and he said to them, "Welcome to Africa, and welcome to Congo. Thank you for coming to our country where we have so many riches, and yet our people live in misery."

I find hope knowing that there are people like Ocean, like Luc, like Jean-Parfait, like Mireille. They are Congolese who have not been swallowed up by the situation in their country, by its corrupt system. They will make things better here. And I have no choice but to take up the challenge and privilege to work alongside them and to believe that they will win.

Hotel Bravo out.

CHAPTER 6

Hope in Zambia

Kabuta

20 April 2005

The MSF office compound at Kashikishi town in Nchelenge District bustles in the morning sun. White land cruisers stand in a row under the overhanging branches of a tall shade tree, their back doors open as they are filled with materials—flip charts for training workshops, medical supplies, cold chain boxes we had to buy in Lusaka, parachecks for malaria testing. And then there's the people—doctors, nurses, clinical officers, counselors, translator, driver. Each land cruiser can hold 11 people, and this one will be full today.

The paved road that brought us here on the two-day trip from Lusaka ends just north of Kashikishi, and then we are on dirt. It is

beautiful here. Lake Mweru glistens on the left, with the high escarpment of the Democratic Republic of Congo just visible on the distant shore. We drive past villages of tiny red-brick huts with conical thatched roofs; tidy and neat, some fronted with beautiful stands of brilliant red flowers. After half an hour we turn in at Kabuta, drive past the low blue and white primary school, and reach the rural health center and our AIDS clinic.

The support group is meeting in a small room in the clinic. These are people from Kabuta who have all tested positive for HIV and are patients at our clinic. We provide a number of them with antiretroviral (ARV) drugs, the

An HIV support group in Kabuta

life-prolonging medicine that can stop an HIV-positive person from contracting AIDS. These are the people who are most concerned about what will happen when we are finally able to hand our program over to Zambia's Ministry of Health, since the ministry charges $12 a month for ARVs and, until a cure is found, patients have to be on ARVs for the rest of their lives.

The MSF counselor is fiercely optimistic. "Abigail," she reminds one of the group members, "why say you are sick when you have HIV? Even though you have the virus you can do anything. When you are sick you can't get up and lie around all day; and you are not in a condition like that." Of course, if the prices for ARVs hadn't been forced down and if generic drugs were not available, there is a good chance that Abigail, and many of the others in the room today, would not just be sick—they would be dead.

These people certainly do not look sick. They are even vibrant enough to have an argument today about the vegetable garden they have been working on as an income-generating project. The argument is over 5,000 kwacha—the equivalent of $1.25, divided among a dozen people—so this heated discussion is about a dime. This is one of those times when my breath is taken away by the differences in our economies.

Later in the morning I sit in on a briefing that Andrea, our doctor from Austria, is giving to the Community Caregivers, a group of volunteers from Kabuta who are helping sick people in their community. Andrea goes over the routine: who gets ARVs; who gets nutritional supplements.

The questions come fast and furious. Why are some ARVs more expensive than others? Are they better quality? What about ARVs from India? What happens to our ARVs if people in your country stop making donations? These are all excellent questions, with no easy answers.

One of the things Andrea wants to talk about is our Well Care Package. We give it to our ARV patients every month. It includes soap, folic acid, multivitamins to slow the spread of the virus, nutritional supplements, oral rehydration salts for severe diarrhea, and six condoms.

"I have a question," says Andrea. "We give this package for one month. Are six condoms enough for one month? Do patients use them?" People are shy with their answers—this is about sex after all, but gradually they let us know that six are not enough.

Then Andrea asks another question. "Do you know about the female condom?" A woman who has sat quietly all morning bursts out, "Aweh!"—then looks suddenly shy at her own boldness.

"Aweh," repeats Andrea with a smile. "I think that means no." And as Andrea talks about the female condom, the room breaks into a low hum of excited chatter at the thought that a woman could have that much control over her body.

This is a fine group. They have volunteered to help their community, visiting patients to make sure they are all right when the medical staff is not present. These are the people who will reap the whirlwind of the AIDS pandemic, either because they will get AIDS or because they will keep their communities going when teachers, nurses, farmers, mothers, and fathers fall sick and die. They are the survivors, and their commitment will keep Kabuta alive.

Kambwala

21 April

Every day, we send two teams out to work at one of Nchelenge's rural health centers. One team goes north, the other goes south. Esther, our doctor for the south team, has been here for almost a year and she has seen some wonderful changes.

"It was so much harder at the beginning," she says, as we wait for patients in the crammed little medical office at the Kambwala rural health center. "People were very suspicious because we were drawing blood and they thought we were drinking it. People were slow to come to us. It was so frustrating."

Esther Mtumbuka, an MSF doctor from Tanzania, counsels HIV/AIDS patients in a rural clinic in Kambwala.

Gradually, the first brave people—often those who were very sick—came for help and we would give them ARVs.

"Once the first people started getting better, leaving their beds and returning to work and to care for their families, then other people started coming to us asking to be tested, asking for CD4 counts, asking for ARVs. It is great when patients start demanding treatment from us," Esther says.

"Before we will put someone on ARVs our counselors talk with them, telling them that ARVs are for life, that they may have side effects like vomiting, dizziness, or diarrhea. We also have to assess their motivation, because they are starting a treatment that they will have to follow for the rest of their lives. So when people say to us, 'I want to see my children grow, I want to run my business,' we know there will be a good chance they will follow the treatment to the letter.

"We had to have meetings with the traditional healers to share our practices, since people with AIDS go to them as well as to us," Esther continues. "We learned that traditional healers will give herbs to encourage diarrhea in the hope of evacuating the virus from the patient's body. But we want the ARVs to stay in a person's body as long as possible so they will be absorbed. We want the traditional healers to refer patients to us—but in return they wanted MSF to refer patients to them. We couldn't do that. But we let the patients choose what works best for them, and I have to say that our biggest supporters are our patients."

Esther and the clinic officer go to work, screening people for malaria, assessing their physical state, sending them to their support group meeting. A new patient comes in, Enock, a young man who is just skin and bones. I cannot imagine how he even made it to the clinic—he came here from Kashikishi, six kilometers away—and now he is lethargic and scared. Gently, Esther and the clinic officer explain things to him.

In the outer office Mary and Ignatius are dispensing ARVs and other medicines to our patients. These people are fishers and farmers, who come in with their babies. One man holds open a dirty old tupperware container and waits for his medicines. Ignatius and Mary often have to cut the pills in half so they can be small enough for children. Nobody is making ARVs for children.

The man with the tupperware container still has some pills in it. "We gave Jack his first week's worth," says Mary, "and then two extra in case he vomited." She looks in the container—just two are left. She is pleased.

As she puts this week's pills in the container, it dawns on me that Jack got his container from us. It has a cardboard divider in the middle, and on one side of the cardboard, there is a felt-pen drawing of the sun for morning and on the other side, a drawing of the moon. Each side shows him what to take in the morning and what to take at night. Mary reviews the medication schedule with Jack. She seems pleased with his adherence—a fancy term for sticking with the pill schedule.

"But how do you know he will adhere?" I ask. "He could just lie to you about his medicines."

"I don't think this will be a problem," Esther responds. "His wife is a patient of ours, and at first he refused to come and be tested to learn his status. But she started getting stronger and he got sick. So he came and asked for medicine. We will follow him closely. For four weeks he comes in every week, and we give him only one week's worth of ARVs. Then, if his adherence is good, we can go up to two weeks' worth and then more. But, yes, I think he will stay with us."

Babies cry. Babies always cry in clinics. It is a good sound—it means they are healthy enough to make noise. We are packed into this small room, crowded around one table. There must be 15 of us—Mary, Ignatius, and Ackim dispensing drugs and about a dozen patients. One woman comes in for her pills, and sighs heavily as she lowers herself onto the bench. Ignatius goes through the drill. "When do you take this pill?" "Six hours." "And when do you take that one?" "Eighteen hours." "Good." But, though her eyes are bright, she is still only skin and bones.

Ackim, an assistant care supporter who is a volunteer from Kambwala, takes a break to chat. "Many people were bed bound and others used to hide away, the stigma was so bad. But then they saw their neighbors getting better so they came here and said to us, 'Give us ARVs now!'

"In the past years there were many deaths. Here a friend, there a friend. Now these have been reduced because of this work here. There were big changes once ARVs started. People overcame their stigma, they would come here time and again," he smiles and points to the table, "because of these drugs." But, of course, let's not forget, these are the privileged few, here in this backwater of Nchelenge District, because most Africans do not have the chance to get ARVs.

This disease is such a deceptive killer. Life here goes on, at least to my eye. The red-brown huts, the lovely thatched roofs, the

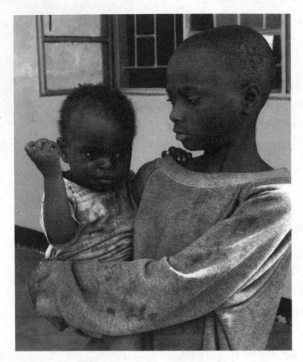

A 12-year-old boy is left caring for his young brother after their parents died of AIDS.

thriving little gardens. There is none of the physical destruction of a war. But last year AIDS killed 1,500 teachers in Zambia, and when that happens in a war, we raise alarm bells because teachers are so important to the health of a society.

Enock, the young man who was just skin and bones, comes to get his first round of medication. Since today is his first day, he does not get ARVs yet. But he does get oral rehydration salts, multivitamins, and a bag of nutritional supplement. Next week we will do his CD4 count and see if he can start ARVs. But as I see him clutching his bags of pills, I wonder how he will be able to cope with all this.

At last he walks laboriously outside into the shaded courtyard and the others in the clinic watch him go as though they are watching a ghost. Outside Enock's father straps the big nutritional supplement bag behind the seat of his bicycle. Enock sits on the ground to watch, then, with considerable effort, he clambers up onto the bag while his father steadies the bike. Then the father and son pedal back towards Kashikishi in the blazing midday sun, taking with them the first tools in that father's long struggle to save the life of his child.

Medical Waste

23 April

Back in the office it is time for the medical meeting, but today's discussion is about a more logistical problem. Waste. Tom, our energetic British logistician, has to figure out how we can safely get rid of all the contaminated materials that are a necessary by-product of any medical program.

Every day we produce hundreds of blood-contaminated needles and vials of blood (called sharps) and rubber gloves and swabs (called softs). We need to find a way to dispose of these in the health clinics in such a way that they are stored forever.

"So," asks Esther, "where can we leave our waste?"

"If the garbage pit is open and has a bunch of kids playing near it, then we will have to bring the waste back here," says Tom. "I would rather not have the waste here, but we have to take responsibility for it. If they have a good pit with a solid lid, then we can use it."

Tom can get enthusiastic about anything, and he takes me to see the pit he has had dug in our office compound. "It's not as good as I would like yet," he says, "but we're getting there. It should be totally bricked down the sides with a solid lid on top so nothing can get in except what we put down there. Then we can also pour concrete in afterward to make sure the bad stuff doesn't find its way out."

There are a number of construction problems we need to address at the rural health centers and Ralph has been tackling these. With plastic pipes and metal fittings, he has designed a safe way to get the needles off the syringes without having to touch them and without, as sometimes happens, the blood spraying back in the nurses' faces. Sometimes it feels that with every step forward a dozen new obstacles suddenly appear. The importance of waste management should have occurred to me, considering there is no garbage pick-up and most health centers only have latrines. It is urgent.

Ralph is a German engineer, and he has been struggling with how to make an incinerator that will melt the needles. He sits at his desk and explains the problems. "There is a standard incinerator for rural health centers, but to get it hot enough for needles would require special glazed bricks to build the hearth. Do you know what they cost? $2.50 per brick and I would have to get them from South Africa. We just can't afford them."

Ralph grows more animated as he talks. "So I thought maybe we could just do a variation on our regular oil-drum incinerators. All you would need is to make the oil drum out of thicker metal. Then I looked on the Internet and I saw there was a company in Uganda that was making incinerator burners hot enough. I e-mailed our logistician in Kampala, she contacted the factory, and from what she says, I think they will be great. She was going to buy one and send it on the bus from Uganda to here—and then just today the bus company refused to transport it." Yet another obstacle. "I've e-mailed Lusaka to see if we can afford to fly it here, but I'm not sure. Maybe I will have to try to design something and ask a factory in Lusaka to try and build a prototype." Ralph shakes his head. "But I'm not sure. I don't know if I can finish the project before I end this mission. I only have five weeks to go."

I saw Ralph the next day at Kambwala. He had come to inspect construction at the rural health center. He is in charge of making more space for the HIV program, since it is crowding out other regular activities there. "We are going to fly the burner in from Kampala," he said happily. "So if it takes a week to get it out of customs and then another week to build the prototype incinerator … I will get this job finished before I have to go home." And the rural health centers will get incinerators that will last.

Kilwa Island

24 April

Early morning on the beach at Boma, and a team is loading our boat with medicine kits. Counselors, clinical officers, doctors, nurses—they all push the boat down the beach and into the lake. Tom works with James, the driver, to balance the load as we prepare for the trip across Lake Mweru to Kilwa Island. Just as we start off, Maggie, one of our counselors, runs across the beach to meet us. It is a close shave, but she will be with us today.

Crossing the lake takes an hour, and we reach Kilwa. Andrea, our Austrian doctor, and the team go into the clinic storeroom for supplies. We fill up containers with malaria parachecks (rapid tests), ARVs, patient files, and cold bags for the CD4 reagents. We carry them back down to the boat under the watching eyes of the mothers and children.

After another 10 minutes on the boat, we arrive at Lukwesa and are met by a welcome party of eight children. Then Duncan, the assistant care supporter, comes up with an elderly woman.

"This grandmother's daughter was HIV-positive, and she died in childbirth. Now this grandmother is looking after the baby." I haven't even noticed the baby, wrapped up in a bundle of old rags. "Now the baby has a fever." Andrea sends the grandmother down to the boat where we have the malaria parachecks, and the grandmother flies off to see if her tiny granddaughter might be helped.

We make our way up the path to the village, and set up in a room of Duncan's thatched-roof home. Patients have heard we are coming and gather on a straw mat in the shade of the mango tree

A child waits for her malaria test.

in front of the house. Malaria is common here, so the first step is to do a rapid test for malaria. While Cletus starts the parachecks, Andrea unpacks her files. In the rafters above our heads, I notice the mattress that Duncan has put up there so we can hold our clinic. We must be in his bedroom.

This is such a labor-intensive way to treat people with AIDS, but at the moment, it is the only way. The team comes over here to this island where, fortunately, rates of infection seem lower than the national average. But if we only do this—provide excellent service and life-prolonging ARVs to AIDS patients—that is just not enough. We must let other HIV-positive people know it is possible to get ARVs, so they will demand the same for themselves.

But there is so much stigma and fear to overcome. "Yesterday I saw a woman in our program along with her baby son," says Andrea. "Her husband died two weeks ago of AIDS-related meningitis. Why didn't he come to see us? He knew his wife and child were HIV-positive. What was going through his mind that stopped him from coming to see us?"

As Andrea and Cletus review patient files, I hear the low drone of our counselor, Jozeph. As he squats in the adjoining room, wearing his shiny green and yellow windbreaker that says Flying Eagles on the back, he talks quietly with the members of the support group of HIV-positive patients.

We look out the window over the thatched-roofed huts down to the lake. It is a picture-postcard view. "You see why I love coming here?" says Andrea. "All in all, you can give really good medicine in a very simple way. I love working with the patients so much."

One patient has a badly abscessed tooth. Any infection can make HIV worse, so we are encouraging her to cross the lake to visit the dentist at St. Paul's in Kashikishi. Since she is one of our patients, we will transport her and pay her medical fees—an important difference in this place where money is barely seen. But she has two children—who will care for them? Cletus says that she would qualify to stay in the shelter for caregivers at St. Paul's. Maybe her children will, too. We weigh and measure her. She is tiny, and we will supply her with the nutritional supplement.

A man comes in next and steps on our bathroom scale to weigh himself. He turns to Andrea and Cletus, smiles, and gives them the thumbs up. "You are doing a commendable job. I am gaining weight."

But he has some serious questions. He is a widower. "Can I marry, with my status?"

Andrea counsels him. "You must inform your partner and always wear a condom."

"But then she will not want to marry me."

"Still, you must inform her, and …," Andrea's voice becomes gentler, "do not plan on having children."

It is so hard to do what must be done to beat this pandemic.

"Mma Muteta," calls Cletus from the window to the next patient waiting outside. Andrea takes Mma Muteta's temperature. "Ah, she is so thin." We weigh her—she is scarcely 31 kilograms (70 pounds)—but her CD4 count is still good, so she is not yet on ARVs.

Mma Muteta needs to go to the dentist. We could take her across to Kashikishi, but her mother has gone to DRC to look for her sister, so no one here can look after her children and she knows no one in Kashikishi.

Five people have turned up today to get tested for HIV, and once they have talked with Jozeph and Maggie to learn how we do the test and why we are taking blood, they come in to see us—women who may get kicked out of their homes if they are positive; a man laughing nervously as he comes for his test. Andrea and Cletus work quickly and diligently, taking blood, writing records. When Kenneth gets back from the other village with the HIV test sticks, we will be able to see if any of these five is HIV-positive.

Before the others return, we have one housebound patient to visit. After a 10-minute walk through the village past huts, fisher-

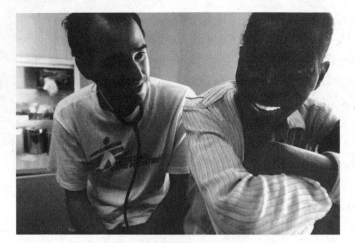

An MSF clinic for HIV/AIDS patients in Zambia

men fixing their nets, kitchen gardens; women and children cooking in the shade, we reach the home of our patient. Her hut is clean and well kept. There is no furniture to speak of in these rooms—a mat, a basket, a log, a stool, a shard of mirror beside a box of matches, and some soap. In the corner of the front room are two pots, a burlap bag of beans, and three squash. The thatch roof and tiny windows keep the house dark and cool despite the midday sun. In front of the house, fish is cooking over a charcoal fire, tended by some children.

Andrea sits on the mat with this patient, trying to make sure that she has not been giving away her medicine to any children. The patient disappears into the back room and brings out her pills in a plastic container. Cletus and Andrea look at her records to figure out how many pills should be left, then count the pills in her container. She has been taking triumune, one of the generic fixed-dose-combination ARVs that have made it so much easier for patients to take their pills correctly. The right number is in her container—she is adhering well.

We need to take more blood to check her CD4 level. She is not happy at this, but consents after we tell her that the CD4 count will tell us how the triumune is working. She screws up her face as Cletus finds the vein to take the blood.

We are very careful as the blood is transfered from the syringe to the vials. Some may say it is not professional to be handling blood specimens like this—taking blood in a hut in a village in a lake in the middle of Africa. I think this is medical professionalism at its height.

The patient has not revealed to her husband that she is HIV-positive. So we ask her, "Don't you think he assumes you are since MSF keeps coming to your house?"

"He just knows I am sick."

"But doesn't he ask why we are coming?" After all, our only program here on Kilwa is HIV/AIDS.

"No," she replies. "He thinks I was very sick. To reveal my status to him would take time. It would just take too long."

"What are you afraid of?" Andrea asks gently.

"There would be no problem. I suggested he go to the Voluntary Testing Center, but he doesn't want to go. He refuses to go. He is afraid to go. He is healthy."

"But if he is positive," Andrea insists, "and he is still healthy, we can help him stay healthy longer. And you need to tell him that with sexual intercourse you can infect each other again. You are getting better with the triumune. If you both join our program, you both have a better chance to live a normal life."

But the patient sits silently, expectantly. She will not tell her husband. The gulf between our different worlds and our different needs is just too great. We are doing what is right for Western medicine, insisting that she tell her husband. She is doing what is right for her—already she has no children, so her status as a wife is precarious to begin with. If he is positive, too, then her husband may well throw her out, and what in the world could an HIV-positive woman with no children do but be an outcast on this beautiful island in the middle of Africa? So her decision not to tell her husband—so wrong in our eyes—is really the only viable option for her.

We walk back through the village to Duncan's house where we left our belongings before heading back to the boat and Kashikishi. Kenneth has returned from the other village and has started the rapid HIV test. He has mixed the blood and the reagent and applied them to the stick. If two lines appear on the stick, then the patient is HIV-positive; if it is only one, she is negative. The tests have been done, and now we wait. In five minutes we will know. We stand around the table, watching the test sticks, and conversation slows as the minutes go by. There are five sticks on the table, five patients, and their family members waiting patiently under the tree outside. Kenneth looks at his watch. Five minutes is up. None of the sticks has two lines. None of these people has HIV. Now how is that for a fantastic day at the office! And as the counselors tell the patients the good news, we repack our gear and head down to the waiting boat to return to Kashikishi.

Scaling Up and Moving On

29 April

If I ever needed convincing, which I didn't, I have been convinced of the importance of this project by my visit here. Off in this neglected corner of Zambia, in the middle of the worst plague the world has seen since the great influenza epidemic, lives are being saved.

It is hard to believe that a year ago Branco Ngosa was on the verge of death, at home alone. Now he is the best advertisement for the services of MSF. He is a dapper man, always well dressed, and today he is wearing a suit and tie.

"Yes, suspicions remain," he says. "People wonder why MSF needs to take blood, and sometimes you forget to tell us why, so rumors start that MSF is drinking the blood or trying to poison us. But I say to people who are afraid to come for counseling and testing, 'Look at me! I was just like you, remember? Don't you want to be like me?' All of us in the Positive Support Group want to encourage other people to get tested so they can be enrolled in the program, too.

"Some people say that MSF is killing people, but I say, no, MSF has given us life." Then he gets a twinkle in his eye. "You know, David," he says, "some people thought MSF must be selling the blood, because how else could you afford to give ARVs for free, hmm?

Phumza Nomnkonko received antiretroviral treatment from MSF in South Africa and is now an HIV-positive volunteer in her community.

"But the chiefs understand now, so that is good. The chiefs saw how AIDS was damaging our community, and now they see that the ARVs are making us stronger again, so they are in favor of the support groups. The chief in Kaputa gave us the land for our community garden."

Free ARVs seem like a dream here. The Ministry of Health people say that they will give free ARVs, but they haven't implemented this yet. The drugs have just come to the district hospital in Nchelenge, but at $12 a month the cost is still very high. And the Nchelenge activists, Branco and the others in the support group, are suspicious. "Even if the Ministry of Health stopped charging," he said in his precise way, "we are unsure that the medicines would reach their intended beneficiaries." In other words, the people in the support group are afraid the medicine would be sold.

David Morley in Zambia

But the stigma in the community is lessening as more people admit to being HIV-positive, and as more people take our ARVs and get better. We even have traditional healers among our patients now.

I have seen posters and wall paintings in every town, on school compound walls, telling Zambians about AIDS and HIV, but still many people seem not to know, or not to believe. Branco and his friends in the support group want to change this, and he smiles his disingenuous smile. "Our future hope is to change Nchelenge into another town. We want to make our community different."

Branco and his group want to plan a demonstration to demand free ARVs for all Zambians. And we have to advocate at home in Canada to get more money into the Global Fund (for AIDS, TB, and malaria), so that poor countries like Zambia can get ARVs. We need to get more generic medicines produced and available so that aid dollars go further, train more health workers, and find ways of ensuring that medicine does not go astray.

People here are anxious about MSF leaving. We remind them that we plan to leave in 2008—that's only three and a half years away. We still have a lot to do if we are to reach that goal—integrating our program with the rural health clinics, advocating for free ARVs with the Zambian government. The estimate is that a million Zambians are HIV-positive, and we are treating only a few hundred people now—a tiny oasis. And so as Maria tries to get a toehold for our program in the Kashikishi Rural Heath Center, as Carina works to make sure the labs at the district hospital keep functioning well, as Ralph waits for his burner and Tom for his next shipment of medicine, as the medical staff keep seeing and treating patients—maybe all their work and the efforts of the national staff will make that oasis grow a little. But then our patients will have to make more noise to make sure that the Zambian government does not squander this opportunity.

I was surprised by hope on my first day in Zambia. I was not prepared for the incredible change that ARVs can make in the lives of people, of communities. People living with AIDS are building futures. If the system works, people will live to see their children grow, they will contribute to their communities. Maybe the tide is turning in places like these villages on the shores of beautiful Lake Mweru, where people like Branco and Jane and Abigail and Ignatius have come back to life, where the six communities of Nchelenge are starting to recover and rebuild. Maybe in the future, when the pandemic has been brought under control, we will remember that this was one of those pioneering places where foreigners and Zambians came together to tackle an insoluble problem, and we won.

INDEX

Photo Credits

Cover (front), Steve Harris; cover (back), Steve Harris; page 3, Steve Harris; p. 5, Didier Lefevre; p. 8, Corbis; p. 10, Corbis; p. 11, Steve Harris; p. 13, Ton Koene; p. 15, Francesco Zizola; p. 18, CP (AP/Jon Eeg); p. 19, Jet Belgraver; p. 23, Steve Harris; p. 24, David Morley; p. 26, Steve Harris; p. 28, Steve Harris; p. 30, Steve Harris; p. 36, Steve Harris; p. 40, Steve Harris; p. 41, Steve Harris; p. 43, Sven Torfinn; p. 45, CP (AP/Adam Butler); p. 46, Steve Harris; p. 47, Corbis; p. 48 top, Steve Harris, p. 48 bottom, Michael Zumstein /L'Oeil Public; p. 49, Remco Bohle; p. 50, Steve Harris; p. 51, Juan Carlos Tomasi MSF; p. 52, Steve Harris; p. 55, Robert Maletta MSF; p. 57, MSF Canada; p. 61, David Morley; p. 63, Roelf Padt MSF; p. 64, MSF; p. 65, Chris Hondros/Getty Images; p. 68, CP (AP/Jockel Finck); p. 72, David Morley; p. 73, CP (AP/Moises Castillo); p. 80, David Morley; p. 81, Steve Harris; p. 82, Steve Harris; p. 85, Steve Harris; p. 87, Steve Harris; p. 88, Steve Harris; p. 89, David Morley; p. 91, David Morley; p. 93, Steve Harris; p 96, Steve Harris; p. 97, Steve Harris; p. 99, Julie Rémy; p. 100, Julie Rémy; p. 103, Julie Rémy; p. 106, CP (AP/Salim Henry); p. 109, Steve Harris; p. 112, Julie Rémy; p. 115, Corbis; p. 116, Jet Belgraver.

Map, pp. 6-7, Paul Heersink, Paperglyphs.